Music in Sequence

A complete guide to MIDI sequencing

William Lloyd and *Paul Terry*

● Musonix Publishing ●

To Lea, Bethan, John
and our friends and students at Kingston Polytechnic
and the City of London Freemen's School

Other music technology titles from Musonix:

Classics in Sequence – A source book for MIDI sequencing
Rock in Sequence – An anthology of pop for sequencing
The Studio Musician's Jargonbuster – A glossary of music technology and recording

First published in 1991
Reprinted with revisions, 1992, 1994, 1996

Published by Musonix Publishing

Exclusive distributors:	Music Sales Corporation	Music Sales Limited	Music Sales Pty.
	257 Park Avenue South	8 / 9 Frith Street	120 Rothschild Avenue
	New York NY 10010 USA	London W1V 5TZ	Rosebery, NSW 2018 Australia

Order Number: MX 30012

Musonix publications are available from The Internet Music Shop: www.musicsales.co.uk

Cover design by Bob Linney

The authors would like to thank Martin Vafadari for his
invaluable contribution to the original music in this book.

Typeset in 11-point Times Roman on Xerox Ventura Publisher™,
with music computer-set in Score™ from Passport Designs, Inc.

Printed and bound in Great Britain by
Caligraving Limited Thetford Norfolk

Contents

What is Sequencing?

Have you ever wished that you could reproduce the sound of a band or orchestra single-handed, adjusting and refining each part as you go?

If you have ever been frustrated by the difficulties of playing an instrument, can you imagine the freedom of being able to record single lines as slowly as you wish, correcting and editing even the tiniest slips before playback?

In both cases, sequencing will provide the answer.

Sequencing is the process of creating music with a little help from a piece of technology called a **sequencer**. This is a device that stores instructions for replaying music on a synthesizer. In effect, a bit like a multi-track tape recorder, but without the tape, and with facilities for editing music that would have been the envy of the biggest recording studio only a few years ago.

Players can produce superbly accurate performances of virtually any kind of music, using a huge range of instrumental sounds.

Composers are, for the first time, able to hear every detail of their work as it is written. The sequencer offers facilities to audition different tone colours, speeds and keys at the touch of a button, and allows sections of the music to be cut, copied and pasted instantaneously into position.

Music in Sequence won't make you into a virtuoso overnight, but will show you how to use the sequencer to take over much of the responsibility for co-ordination and control, allowing you freedom to think musically from the very beginning.

Using this book

Each chapter of **Music in Sequence** is designed like a recipe, taking you step-by-step through all the stages needed to sequence a complete piece of music, from setting-up to finished play-back. Although we have anticipated that most users will input music data from a keyboard, *any* MIDI musical instrument may be used for the sequences in this book.

We do not presuppose any familiarity with either music notation or technology, although complete beginners may find it useful to read the Fact Sheets following this introduction before embarking upon Sequence 1. If you do not yet own any music technology the notes on types of sequencer and synthesizer may guide you towards a user-friendly choice.

Most importantly, do not rush this book! It does not have to be skimmed through in an evening, any more than the entire contents of a guide to world cuisine would be welcome at a single dinner party. We hope that you enjoy it.

Music Systems

Many users of this book will already be familiar with much of the information given here. It has not been sponsored by a manufacturer and will therefore not be recommending particular brands of equipment. Such choices are better made by reading music technology magazines or, better still, by trying out models in a specialist shop where questions can be answered more easily. In fact, surprisingly little equipment is needed to produce high-quality sequenced music, certainly not the van loads of gear which seem to accompany even a small band on tour. Sequencing is largely a creative process and, unless you want your work to be audible in the next street but one, it is possible to put together a perfectly usable system relatively cheaply.

WHAT YOU NEED

Multi-timbral synthesizer
Computer, MIDI interface and sequencer software
Powered monitor speaker(s) or headphones
MIDI and audio leads

Powered monitors (also known as keyboard amplifiers) are heavy-duty loudspeakers with built-in amplification. If you have a synthesizer with stereo outputs you will ideally need two monitors. Using a hi-fi amplifier and speakers is not recommended as they can easily be damaged by the peak output levels of a synthesizer.

Atari ST computers are very widely used for sequencing in Europe and accordingly have a large range of music software available.

There are many sequencer programs available for all of the popular microcomputers, varying in price and sophistication. Most require the use of a mouse. The MIDI interface is essential, but has to be purchased as an extra for almost all computers other than the Atari ST series.

Sequencers are also available as stand-alone units and as part of many multi-timbral synths. However, a computer-based sequencer offers greater flexibility as well as the advantage of a large screen display and easier controls. Wiring up should be done as follows:

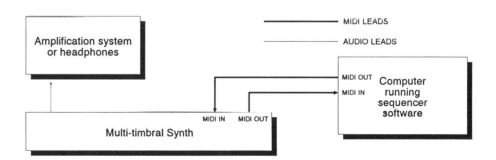

A **multi-timbral** synth is able to play a number of different instrumental sounds (**voices**) simultaneously. You may already have access to a synth which can use only one voice at a time. Such **mono-timbral** instruments can also be used for sequencing, particularly if extra synths (or a rack module) plus a drum machine are added to the system to give multi-timbral capability:

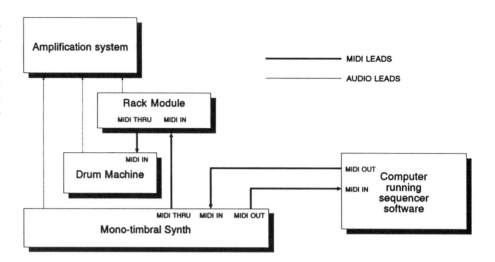

Note that this set-up works well for sequencing, although you may not be able to play the rack module directly from the keyboard unless your sequencer offers a software MIDI Thru facility. This, like an actual MIDI Thru output, simply relays data on unchanged from the MIDI In socket.

MIDI

Central to any music technology system is the ability of its component pieces of equipment to communicate with each other. This is done primarily using a simple electronic link known as **MIDI** (Musical Instrument Digital Interface).

MIDI allows vital music information, such as the pitch, volume, start and end of notes, to be transmitted numerically from keyboard to syntheziser or between synths. MIDI data can also be generated by wind and string players, guitarists and drummers using suitably equipped instruments. There is even a MIDI mike for singers. Most importantly, MIDI information can be stored, edited and arranged for playback, using a device known as a **sequencer**.

SYNTHESIZERS

Basically a **synthesizer** is an electronic sound generator having in its memory the information needed to create the characteristics of a number of acoustic and electric sounds. All of these **voices** can be edited by the user, so in theory the sound of a piano can be transformed into the noise of an atomic explosion. In practice, radical voice editing is seldom needed by the musician as there are now thousands of extra sounds available for the more popular synths.

The keyboard and synthesizer are actually two separate components, although often both are housed in the same unit. However, synths are also available in compact form without keyboards (rack modules) as are keyboards without any sound-generating facilities of their own (master keyboards). A few synths can even be bought as circuit boards for direct insertion into a computer.

To avoid the need for more than one instrument, most synthesizers are now multi-timbral, allowing a number of different voices to be played simultaneously across the entire pitch range. This is an enormous bonus for the musician who wishes to reproduce the sounds of a complete ensemble without having hardware stacked throughout the house.

With only one pair of hands, however, it is virtually impossible to play more than one or two voices at a time without a means of storing MIDI information elsewhere for simultaneous playback. This is one of the main functions of the sequencer *(see opposite)*. Many people who use multi-timbral synths merely as performing keyboards are often unaware of the full range of facilities at their disposal.

WORKSTATIONS

Some manufacturers have developed **workstations**, providing virtually a complete sound studio in a single box. These add effects such as reverb and delay, drum kits and an on-board sequencer to the basic multi-timbral synth and keyboard. The tiny visual display of most workstations, however, means that when sequencing you will probably get better results and less eye-strain using a separate computer-based sequencer.

OTHER OPTIONS

A single **mono-timbral** synth can be used to record and play the sequences in this book: the main drawback is that only one voice is available at any given time. This problem can be side-stepped by recording each part separately onto a multi-track tape recorder synchronized with the sequencer. If this proves too laborious, it may be easier simply to play back the sequences using the same voice for all parts.

SEQUENCERS

A sequencer is a device or computer program for storing and manipulating MIDI data. Many sequencers seem to operate like a multi-track tape recorder, but it is important to realize that the "recording" is not of actual sound but of performing instructions for a synth or other MIDI device.

The sequencer is, however, much more flexible than the tape recorder. Not only can you jump to any part of the music instantly, without having to wait for the tape to rewind, but you also get an automatic graphic representation of what you have played.

Because MIDI information is numeric, you can edit any part of the recording without recourse to the traditional razor blade. Furthermore, some sequencers will display MIDI data in a form of traditional music notation and allow you to print it out.

Music can be recorded at any speed, however slow – faster playback will not affect the pitch of notes. Complex textures can be built-up layer by layer and mistakes are easily corrected. You don't have to be a perfect musician in order to create a perfect performance.

Using The System

MIDI CHANNELS

Sequencers allow you to record music on different tracks so that you can separate the parts intended for different voices. The synth has only one MIDI input, however, and it requires a means of deciphering which notes are to be played by each voice. The data for each track is therefore identified by a MIDI **channel** number. This is recognized by the synth, just as a television set can distinguish between signals from many different TV channels (although, unlike the television, synths can respond to all channels simultaneously):

Parallel information cannot pass down a single lead simultaneously. In fact, it is sent serially, but so quickly that the ear does not notice any time lapse.

Tracks and channels set on sequencer   Tracks and voices set on synth combination

SETTING UP THE SYNTH

Multi-timbral synths can be set to a single voice for live performing or to a multi-timbral **combination** (also called a multi-patch or configuration) ready to play several voices at once. There are several types of combination designed for live playing, including split keyboard (different voices for left and right hands), layered (two or more voices playing the same notes) and velocity sensitive (the voice changes with a firmer key pressure).

For sequencing, however, you will need a **multi-channel** combination for receiving data on several different MIDI channels. It doesn't matter which voices are preset, as these can be changed from the sequencer. In fact, only one combination is needed for all your sequencing and this should be as uncluttered as possible.

If your synth does not offer such a preset, create your own as follows:

1. Find a preset combination that you don't mind altering.

2. Set a multi-channel combination and assign each of the voices within it to a separate MIDI channel (generally there will be 8 or 16 voices to assign).

3. Select a clear voice for each channel. It is unimportant precisely which sounds you choose, as each sequence will reset this part of the combination.

4. Make sure each voice is set to maximum output level, with no transposition, and will operate over the entire pitch range (*ie* not limited by a "window").

5. Each voice should have MIDI program, controller and aftertouch enabled (MIDI filters off) as these are features required by later sequences in this book.

6. Features such as detuning (thickening of sound), effects (*eg* reverb) and panning to left or right can be set for each voice as desired.

7. Re-name the combination and save it in the synth's internal memory.

This may all seem frighteningly complicated. However, getting a usable combination set up now will save you hours of time later on and, of course, it only ever has to be done once.

There is one other potential pitfall when voicing from the sequencer. In multi-timbral mode the synth uses one channel (known sometimes as the global channel) for operations which affect the instrument as a whole. This global channel is usually MIDI Channel 1, although it can be reassigned if you wish. A voice number set on the sequencer for this channel may well throw the synth into the wrong combination. No sequence in this book uses more than seven different voices simultaneously, so it may generally be easier to use Channel 2 and above for sequencing, while reserving Channel 1 for auditioning voices on the keyboard.

SETTING UP A DRUM KIT

Unlike most other voices, individual drum sounds play at fixed pitches. This means that a number of different sounds, each with its own MIDI note number, are grouped together as one voice on many synths. You will therefore need to know which note plays, say kick drum or cymbal, before you can write drum parts on the sequencer. A list will almost certainly be supplied with your synth.

DRUM MACHINES

While the drum kit on a synth provides many useful sounds, it cannot supply any automatic rhythm patterns. A drum machine is a synthesizer programmed to produce percussion sounds which it can store as short, sequenced patterns. The drum parts given in this book have been designed to fit with the musical style of each piece and can be written onto a drum machine or recorded on the sequencer using the synth's drum kit.

If you use a separate drum machine it will need to be synchronized with the sequencer so that the rhythm of a song does not come adrift. This is done using one of the several synchronization systems offered on most sequencers. The easiest to use is probably MIDI clock. Check that the sequencer is set to *Sync: Internal* and the drum machine to *Sync: Midi* (or vice-versa) on playback.

METRONOME

Sequencers organize the MIDI information they receive using the system of bars and beats found in music. The speed is set before recording and a metronome beat is provided to keep you in time. Playing to the metronome takes a bit of practice but is essential if the track is to synchronize with previously recorded material. It is also necessary if you want to be able to locate precise parts of the music on the sequencer.

PLAYBACK OPTIONS

As well as listening to all parts at once it is possible to **solo** an individual track for checking or to **mute** specific tracks while working on voicing. Sections of the complete mix or, on certain sequencers, single tracks, can also be **looped** (or cycled) for repetitive playback.

PATTERNS

Some sequencers expect you to divide the music into short sections called **patterns**, which can be separately named, edited and saved. It is much quicker when copying if patterns are multiples of complete bars. This is best done by setting in advance the exact end-point of a pattern before recording into it.

COMPUTER TIPS

Make a copy of your sequencer program before first using it and set the write-protect slider on these disks to prevent accidental erasure. Sequenced music should be saved to separate working and back-up disks at frequent intervals. These precautions provide a safety net in the event of computer, power or user failure! Save each sequence under an easily identifiable name.

Sequences are normally saved as complete songs, not individual patterns, using the sequencer's own internal format. If you want to transfer your work onto a different type of sequencer you will need to use the MIDI song file format. Note, however, that disks from one type of computer will not usually work on another unless it is known that the two are compatible.

There is a growing problem with computer "viruses" – small programs, concealed on disk, that are designed to spoil the operation of legitimate software, often destroying valuable data in the process. You can minimize the risk of "infection" by ensuring that no disk is loaded into your computer unless you are entirely confident of its previous history and whereabouts. This is particularly important if your system contains a hard disk.

Getting Started
Sequencer Screens

The graphic below is the "front page" of a typical computer sequencer. No actual sequencer looks exactly like this; every manufacturer strives to make the look and feel of their product a little different from rival programs. All sequencers, however, have many features in common. If you are new to sequencing, or even to computers in general, finding the various functions is much easier if you know what you are looking for and have some idea of how it might be displayed.

We have all, at some stage, had to load an unfamiliar program and then stumble around trying to find out how it is organized. Computer manuals are not renowned for their clarity and can often read as though they have been translated by someone with no knowledge of the language, the program, or both! If you can find a section in the manual headed **Your First Recording** or **Instant Gratification**, turn to it with relief. If not, the basic features shown here may help to point you in the right direction.

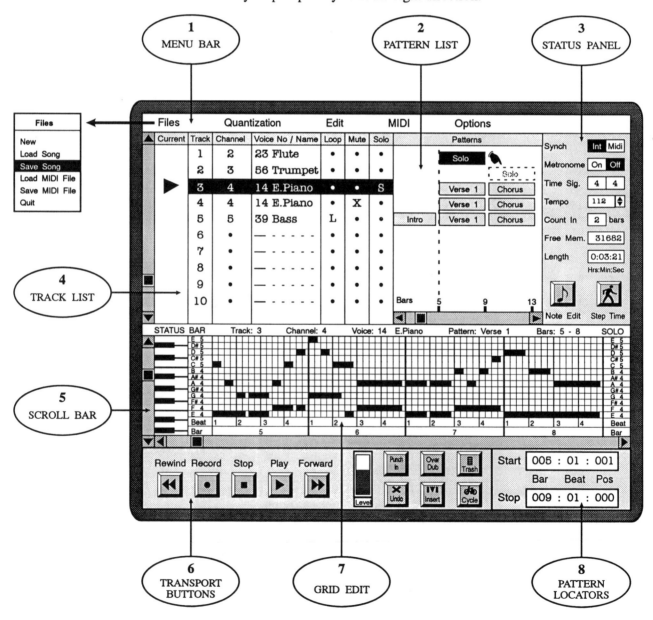

COMMON FUNCTIONS

You will need some familiarity with the basic functions of the sequencer program before you can make your first recordings. Virtually all sequencers provide similar features to the ones shown *opposite*. Most "main screens" seem complex at first sight because programmers try to ensure that as many functions as possible are immediately to hand. The areas of operation ringed on the diagram will be found on most sequencers using similar, if not identical, terminology.

1 Highlighting words on the **Menu Bar** causes a drop-down menu to appear, giving a further range of editing and other options.

2 The **Pattern List** allows you to name, edit and move some sections of a track without affecting others.

3 The **Status Panel** shows how the sequencer is currently set-up.

4 Synthesizer voice numbers, MIDI channels and other functions affecting individual tracks are selected in the **Track List**.

5 **Scroll Bars** are used to reach parts of the display not currently in view.

6 Moving to different sections of the music is usually done by a system of **Transport Buttons** which simulate the controls on a tape recorder.

7 The **Grid Edit** is one of the most useful part of the program, providing a precise graphic display of the music, with all the tools needed for editing it. Grid Edit displays vary greatly: all show note-lengths although pitch data is sometimes relegated to a list at the side of the grid. The relationship between traditional music notation and the grid display can be seen in many of the sequences in this book, and particularly in the example on page 40.

8 Some sequencers have **Pattern Locators** in order to set exact start and end points for recording and playback.

MOUSE TECHNIQUE

Most programs use the computer's **mouse** to move a pointer around the screen. Clicking the left mouse button on the screen icons activates or de-activates the various options. Variable values, such as Tempo (speed) or Bar Position can generally be increased or decreased by holding down the left or right button. Beginners should note that clicking at random around the screen can easily result in dramatic unplanned changes to the music.

The computer keyboard is used for typing information such as instrument names or song titles. Also, it will often provide short cuts for various time-consuming mouse functions. A list of these options will certainly be hidden somewhere in the manual.

Many programs make use of a technique called "dragging" for moving information around the screen. This involves clicking on an item to highlight it (such as the Flute Solo pattern in black on the diagram). The left mouse button is then held down while the item is dragged to a new location, such as the Trash Can for deletion. On the screen, the Flute Solo pattern is shown being moved to bar nine on the Trumpet track - the mouse pointer changes to a hand and the pattern is shown in faint outline as it is being moved.

Reading the Dots

These pages contain some brief reminders of basic note-reading skills. For all its imprecision, traditional notation remains the most practical and widely understood way of writing music data. If you are keen to get started, skip over this section and come back to it if you have difficulty with the music in the sequences. Theory on its own can be a chore: however, if you use notation regularly you'll find the skills will come naturally.

RHYTHM

Rhythm, quite simply, is the effect produced by the interaction of a steady **beat** (pulse) overlaid by the individual lengths of each note. This beat is given by the metronome on the sequencer and is grouped into **bars**, often of 3 or 4 beats.

In music notation, bars are shown by vertical lines across the music called **bar-lines**. Any note on the first beat of each bar (the one that immediately follows each bar-line) is usually played with a stronger pulse than the others.

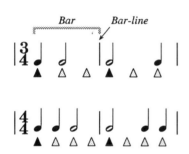

In the music itself the beat may actually be played by an instrument such as the kick drum, but often it is more subtle and is only *felt* through the accurate placing of each individual note rather than being specifically audible.

The number of beats contained in each bar is shown by the upper figure of the **time signature** (eg $\frac{3}{4}$ - three beats in a bar). The lower figure, usually 4, means that the beat consists of quarter-notes. An 8 at the bottom would indicate a pulse written in eighth-notes.

In music notation, **note lengths** are distinguished by different shapes of notes. The sequencer's grid, more helpfully, displays the actual lengths:

Groups of eighth- and sixteenth-notes are usually beamed together into one-beat units.

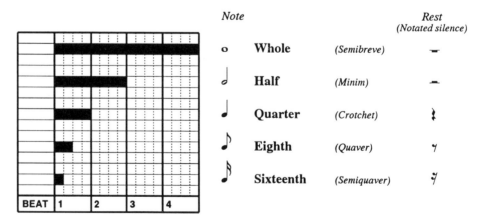

Note			Rest (Notated silence)
o	Whole	*(Semibreve)*	⎯
♩	Half	*(Minim)*	▬
♩	Quarter	*(Crotchet)*	𝄽
♪	Eighth	*(Quaver)*	𝄾
♬	Sixteenth	*(Semiquaver)*	𝄿

English note lengths *(minim, crotchet, etc)* are shown here for reference, but sequencers have adopted the more logical system of half-notes and quarter-notes found in most other countries and used throughout this book.

4-beat rest   3-beat rest

The whole-note rest has an additional function: it is also used to indicate a **whole bar** rest in any time. So, the length of the symbol shown *left* varies according to the time-signature.

$\frac{1}{2} + \frac{1}{4}$ $1 + \frac{1}{2}$

Longer note-lengths can be made by placing a **dot** *after* existing notes. This has the effect of increasing their lengths by 50%. So, a dotted half-note will last for three beats and a dotted eighth-note will last for ¾ of a beat *(see left)*.

$1 + \frac{1}{4}$ $1 + 1$

Other note-lengths can be obtained by linking two notes together with a curved line called a **tie**. This is essential if a note has to be extended beyond a bar-line.

In reality, notes are often played shorter than their notation would suggest. However, it is important for rhythm to sound tight by ensuring that notes *start* at their correct place in the bar.

Andante	*Fairly slow*	*72 bpm*
Moderato	*Moderate*	*84 bpm*
Allegro	*Fast*	*108 bpm*
Vivace	*Lively*	*126 bpm*
Presto	*Very fast*	*144 bpm*
Rit. or Rall.	*Slowing down*	
Accel.	*Speeding up*	
A Tempo	*Back to speed*	

The effect of rhythm patterns will be influenced by the **tempo** chosen. This is often left to the performer to decide, although sometimes composers will give a vague indication at the start – *slow rock* or *lively.* Traditionally, these speed markings were written in Italian. A selection is given, *left*, with an approximate indication of the beats per minute (**bpm**) which the sequencer requires.

Sometimes the speed of the piece is given in the form of a metronome mark **M.M.** ♩ **= 120** which is the exact equivalent of a bpm setting.

Choosing the right tempo is one of the musician's most important artistic decisions.

NOTE NAMES

The white notes on the keyboard are named with the seven letters A to G. On the eighth note the series A-G starts again, but in a new octave. Sequencers and synths identify the different octaves by number, but there is more than one system and they will not necessarily line up. If C3 on the keyboard registers as C5 on the sequencer, you will have some simple maths to do!

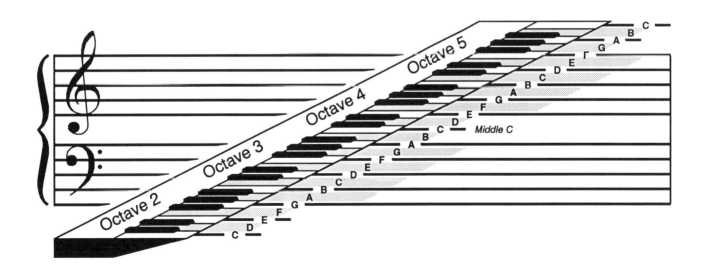

If you are new to music reading, some self-adhesive labels on the synth keys (perhaps just on C, E and G) may help you find and memorize the note names.

STAVES AND CLEFS

The five lines on which music is written is called a **stave**. The **treble** and **bass clefs** at the start of each stave are medieval versions of the letters G and F, reminding you of the location of these notes on the stave. Keyboard music generally uses a bass stave for the left hand and a treble stave for the right.

ACCIDENTALS

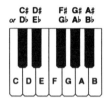

The names of the black keys are either raised or lowered versions of their adjacent white notes. A **sharp** (♯) is just above the normal note and a **flat** (♭) is just below. A **natural** (♮) cancels the effect of a sharp or flat. If such changes are only needed on a temporary basis, they are indicated by one of these signs (collectively known as **accidentals**) before the note. Accidentals apply to all remaining similar notes in the bar, which is why the fourth note here is still F-sharp but the last note is F-natural because it is in a new bar:

KEY SIGNATURES

When a piece needs sharps or flats throughout, they are not written into every bar as temporary accidentals. They appear instead as a **key signature** at the start of each stave. The first key signature on the left means that every B in the piece (whatever the octave) should be played as B-flat, while the second means that every F becomes an F-sharp.

TONES AND SEMITONES

A **semitone** is the jump from one note to the *very* next note. C to C# is a semitone, so is D to E-flat. E to F is also a semitone, as there is no black note between. A **tone** is two semitones: C to D is a tone, and so is E-flat to F.

INTERVALS

There are two different systems for measuring the distance between notes of different pitch. Musicians tend to think in terms of **intervals**, counting up the notes of the scale using the method to the left, below. A more precise technique is used by sequencers, which work in semitone steps, as shown to the right. The vital difference is that intervals reckon on the base note as one, while semitone steps assume it to be zero:

The
Sequences

Sequence 1
Basic Patterns

All music, however complex it may finally appear, is constructed from fundamentally simple units. These may consist merely of a few notes of melody, a short rhythm pattern or a series of chords. Like an architect with the raw materials for building, the musician's task is to manipulate, combine and transform these basic ideas into a musical structure. The sequencer allows all of these functions to be performed at the touch of a button. It can therefore revolutionize the process of composing for those who wish to write their own music as well as provide a means of playing music which would otherwise be impossible. Sequence 1 is about creating these basic patterns and using the sequencer to combine and transform them.

The Plan

> A **riff** is a short, regular pattern that can be repeated at different pitches to form the basis of a longer piece.

To record a two-bar chord pattern of two-beat notes played in time with the metronome. Then to add a bass track in a different rhythm and use the sequencer to extend and transform this material into a 16-bar **riff**. Finally, to add a simple drum track.

The Method

CHORDS TRACK

➠ Set your synth to a multi-timbral combination number (see page 8).

➠ Set the sequencer as follows:
  Track 1   **Midi Channel 2**   **Piano**

You will need to know the program or voice numbers of the piano sounds on your synth. One of these numbers should be set for Track 1 on the sequencer, so that it will set this voice on the synth. Sequencers have different ways of entering program information. Check your manual for details.

It is a good idea to name each track (or pattern) for easy identification when editing. Before voicing or naming a track, you may have to initialize it by creating an empty pattern for recording.

➠ Check that the metronome is on and the time-signature set for 4/4 time.

➠ Set the tempo to record at a comfortable speed – say, 100 bpm.

➠ Set a bar or two of lead-in to give the tempo before you start recording.

> **Chords** are notes intended to be sounded together.

Record the following chords track, making sure that all three notes of each chord go down together. It can be played using either both hands or, preferably, with just the right hand and the fingering (see page 21) shown:

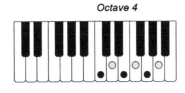

Octave 4

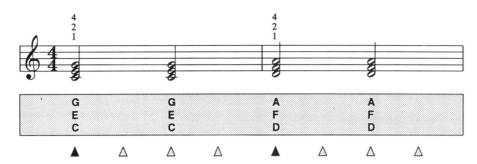

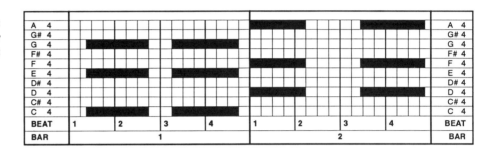

➡ Listen back. Look at the **grid edit** screen. You should see the chords starting on, or close to, beats 1 and 3 in each bar, as follows:

Sequencers display note data in a variety of ways. Some may show only one bar at a time or produce a vertical grid.

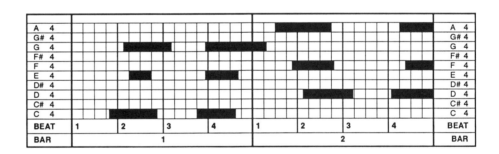

QUANTIZATION

If the notes are *slightly* out of position, the sequencer can nudge them to the nearest beat. This process is called **quantization**. However, if your chords are as far from the beat as these are .....

..... quantization will move them to the wrong beat entirely. You should either re-record them, playing more rhythmically, or mouse them into their correct positions on the grid. If your sequencer has a music display you will be able to see that where you thought you played four even chords, the sequencer has recorded four very complex-looking rhythms, something like this:

This is because notation is only a *guide* to playing, but sequencers have a ruthless logic that makes a *literal* interpretation of performance data. It also shows why it is easier to edit music on the grid rather than on the music display!

➥ Quantize the track to *quarter notes*. Any rogue notes will be moved automatically to their correct positions, thus:

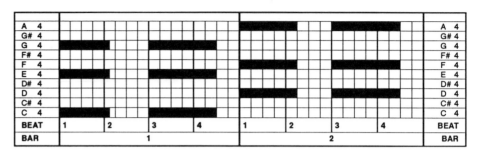

The chords are now in the right position but quantization has not altered their lengths. This reflects a natural way of playing: making note lengths totally even can produce a tediously regular performance. Since most musical sounds die away it is the *start* of each chord that you will notice more than the end.

Remember, it is VITAL to save your work to disk at frequent intervals. Many a fine sequence has been lost by those who forget!

➥ Listen back to check that quantization has tightened the rhythm. **Save it!**

BASS TRACK

➥ Mute Track 1 and set the sequencer for:

| Track 2 | Midi Channel 3 | Synth Bass |

Make certain that you *have* moved to Track 2 or you will erase the work already recorded.

➥ Check that the metronome and lead-in are still set, as before, and record the following bass track. The first note lasts for 7 beats (4 + 3):

Octave 2

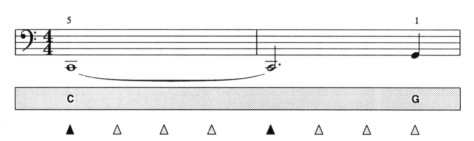

➥ Save your work, switch Track 1 back on and listen to both tracks together.

➥ Quantize the bass track to quarter-notes if it does not synchronize with the chords. The metronome and lead-in will not be needed from now on.

TRANSFORMATIONS

The next stage is to extend this material to 16 bars by a process of copying.

Some sequencers may allow both tracks to be copied simultaneously.

➥ Copy the existing two-bar chord pattern into bars 3 and 4 on **Track 1**.

➥ Repeat the process for the bass pattern on **Track 2**.

The resulting four bars is a useful pattern length for many types of music.

➥ Now copy the four-bar pattern three times to fill bars 5-16 on each track:

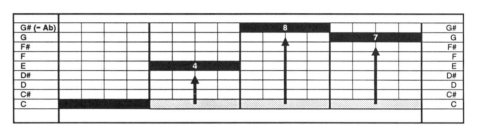

➥ Save it to disk. Winch up the tempo to something livelier and listen back.

Transposition is the process of shifting the pitch of a pattern up or down into a new key.

Even at a faster speed, you will probably agree that the sequence still sounds repetitive. Rather than introducing new material at this stage, it is a more effective technique to **transpose** some of the existing music.

➥ Transpose bars 5-8 of both tracks up four semitone steps. This will effectively shift these bars into the key of E.

➥ Repeat the process for bars 9-12, this time transposing up eight semitones, moving the pattern to the key of A-flat .

➥ Transpose the last four bars up seven semitones to the key of G.

➥ Save it! **Loop** (cycle) both tracks and listen back.

DRUM TRACK

Finally, to add a simple drum track. If you have a separate drum machine you may prefer to select an appropriate pattern, set the drum machine's clock to MIDI and simply trigger the pattern from your sequencer. Or you could write the pattern given *overleaf* directly into the drum machine.

Drum tracks usually consist of short, repetitive patterns that need to be very precise rhythmically. This is the ideal opportunity to use **step time** writing, which gives excellent control over note positioning, although it is often too slow to use for long musical patterns.

➥ First check that you have a drum kit properly set up, as explained on page 8, and that you have a note of which pitch will play each instrument in the kit if your sequencer needs this information. As this will vary according to the type of synth you use, note pitches are not given in this section.

➥ Set the sequencer for:

Track 3	Midi Channel 4	Drum Kit

In **step time** writing you can record individual notes at your leisure. It is a useful alternative to **real time** recording in which you have to keep playing in time, albeit at a very slow pace if you wish.

➥ Move to the **drum edit** screen if your sequencer has one. Otherwise move into your sequencer's **step time** mode – on many sequencers this is simply the usual grid edit screen, on which you place notes by clicking with the mouse. Some sequencers may insist that you insert a couple of blank bars into which you can insert notes.

The foundation of the drum kit, live or electronic, is the **kick drum** *(bass drum)* which often plays a simple pattern of 2 or 4 notes per bar. Start this two-bar drum pattern by inserting notes for kick drum on beats 1 and 3 of both bars, thus:

Kick Dr																	Kick Dr
BEAT	1		2		3		4		1		2		3		4		BEAT
BAR				1								2					BAR

Most drum sounds are actually very short, but music notation conventionally shows these notes as one-beat long to avoid a complex-looking layout. Once again, it is the starting position of the note that is critical, not the precise length.

To give some drive to the rhythm, add four notes for **snare drum** on the **off-beats** (that is, beats 2 and 4), giving a small jolt to the pattern by putting the second of these half a beat later than the others:

Snare Dr																	Snare Dr
Kick Dr																	Kick Dr
BEAT	1		2		3		4		1		2		3		4		BEAT
BAR				1								2					BAR

➡ Save your work. Loop or copy the drum pattern – it doesn't need to be transposed like the other tracks – and listen back to the finished sequence.

Developments

Sequence 1, like many of the sequences in this book, is capable of further development. The purpose of this section is to suggest some possible ideas which may act as a trigger for your own explorations.

Many sequencers let you change voices "on the fly" as the music is cycling, so that you can audition a range of possible sounds.

For example, you may wish to experiment with faster speeds or different voicings – a clearer bass sound or a more sustained voice for the chords. It is quicker to do this by changing voices from the sequencer rather than re-setting the synthesizer.

You could also add a melodic motif on a new track, such as the following:

It will need to be copied and transposed in the same way as Tracks 1 and 2 and suitably voiced using a new MIDI channel. This could provide a good opportunity to explore some of the more remote reaches of your synthesizer's voice list!

Playing The Keyboard

*All keyboard players gradually develop a technique for playing which is uniquely their own. The term **technique** is often misused to imply something separate from the artistic elements of performance. In reality, it is simply the ability of the hands, arms and brain to be able to fulfil the player's musical demands. It is not the purpose of this book to set out a list of rules which must be followed at all costs. However, certain guidelines may prove helpful, particularly for the beginner.*

TYPES OF KEYBOARD

Many players, especially those who are already used to the piano, will find that most synthesizer keyboards require surprisingly little weight to depress the keys. Because of this it is easy to play so hard that all aspects of touch sensitivity are registered at maximum by the synthesizer, preventing any variety of volume or tone. Some players prefer the "feel" of a weighted keyboard, which offers more resistance to the fingers.

SITTING OR STANDING

The structure of muscles in the wrist and arm makes it easier to sit, particularly now that keyboards are so responsive to finger pressure. It is more difficult to make much variation in tone when standing up, in spite of the visual advantages in live performance. With the hand bent back at an angle from the forearm, the wrist will not be able to move freely and the playing will risk sounding lumpy and uncontrolled.

A comfortable sitting position at the right height for the keyboard is essential if you are going to spend hours in the studio, especially if you are also constantly reaching for the mouse and other sequencer controls. Preventing muscular tension and discomfort is one of the main tasks facing the performer.

TOUCH SENSITIVITY

Most synth keyboards are able to register key pressure. Try targeting a range of velocity levels with each finger in turn. Ideally, all ten fingers should become equally efficient at playing. Get to know the responses of various voices: sensitivity will vary widely from nil on, say, **organ** to the volatile reactions of a **sax** sound.

AFTERTOUCH

If you press harder into the key, many synths also register **aftertouch** as the sound continues. This modifies the tone, and sometimes the loudness or pitch, of certain voices as decided by the programmer.

FINGERING

The fingers of each hand are numbered, as shown *right*. To avoid moving the hand around too much, you will often need to use all five fingers when playing a track. Comfortable fingerings for doing this are sometimes shown by numbers above or below the notes in keyboard music.

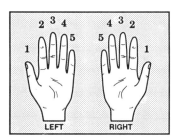

Sequence 2
Beats and Pulses

*A regular, rhythmic beat is the engine of music just as a regular heart rate is the engine of life. Like the human heart, the basic underlying beat of music is often called the **pulse**. It runs faster when the mood is exciting and the adrenalin pumping, and more slowly when we relax. Small variations in the regularity of the pulse make music interesting and exciting – but major hesitations and stops can herald breakdowns and the ultimate collapse of the performance. Fortunately, the sequencer is an electronic pace-maker. It forces the pulse rate to become even and to keep going, thus overcoming this greatest of obstacles for all musicians in the early stages. Sequence 2 is about responding to this regular beat in various ways, using the sequencer's metronome as a guide.*

The Plan

To create a bass track with a regular beat, played in time with the metronome. Then to explore placing notes before and after the beat, both in real time and step time, when adding drum, melody and rhythm tracks. Finally, to use the sequencer to cut and paste patterns to create fresh material.

The Method

BASS TRACK

➡ Set your synthesizer to the combination used in Sequence 1.

➡ This time, set the sequencer as follows:

| Track 1 | Midi Channel 2 | Any decent bass sound |

➡ Check that the metronome is on, with a bar or two of lead-in. Record at a comfortably slow speed, say, 60 bpm.

Record the following bass track, making sure that both notes of each chord go down together. It can be played either using both hands or preferably with just the left hand and the fingering shown. Start on the lowest G on the keyboard:

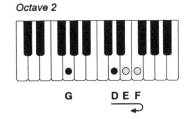

Octave 2

G D E F

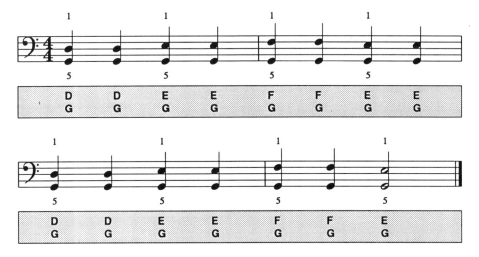

➥ Look at the grid. The first two bars should resemble the following:

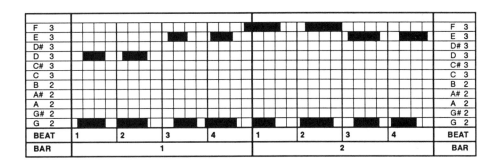

➥ Quantize the track to *quarter-notes* to nudge the chords onto the beat.

The principle behind quantization is that the sequencer moves every note to the nearest beat you specify: in this case, onto the quarter-note beats. This always means that any notes within 50% (*ie* an eighth-note) of their true position will be moved correctly, while any notes further out of time than this will get moved onto the wrong beat. If quantization produces an unsatisfactory result, the track can either be carefully re-recorded at a slower speed or individual offending notes can be edited into position on the grid.

Most sequencers also offer a percentage quantize for occasions when 100% transformation would be too radical.

➥ Double the tempo setting to 120 bpm and set the track to loop. Save your work and listen back.

DRUM TRACK

As before, if you have a drum machine you may prefer to use a preset pattern or you may wish to write the pattern given here directly on the drum machine.

➥ Be certain you move to **Track 2** and set the sequencer for:
Track 2   **Midi Channel 3**   **Drum Kit**

➥ Move into **step time** or to the **drum edit** screen if your sequencer has one.

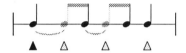

As in Sequence 1, the **kick drum** will provide a steady background beat of four notes per bar. However, four quarter-notes in every bar can become a bit too regular, so insert the first and last notes on beats 1 and 4 as usual, but this time try placing the second and third notes two-sixteenths late, on the **off beat**:

Kick Dr						→				→						Kick Dr
BEAT	1				2				3				4				**BEAT**

➡ Loop the track and listen back.

➡ Next add four notes for **hand claps**, one on each beat. This time try moving a couple of them one-sixteenth *before* the beat to produce **syncopation**.

Claps				←									←				Claps
Kick Dr																	Kick Dr
BEAT	1				2				3				4				**BEAT**

Notice how the music notation shows the off-beat and syncopated notes. It looks complex because, unlike the grid, overlapping notes are not used. Instead, adjacent notes must be shortened or lengthened to preserve the pattern of four beats in the bar.

➡ Finally, add *two* groups of four sixteenth-notes for **closed hi-hat**, precisely in the positions shown below:

Cl. HiHat																	Cl. HiHat
Claps																	Claps
Kick Dr																	Kick Dr
BEAT	1				2				3				4				**BEAT**

➡ Loop the track and listen back. The two groups of **hi-hat** notes should sound different, although they both consist of the same four notes, because the first group starts *on* a beat while the second starts on an *off* beat.

MELODY TRACK

The art of writing a good piece is in striking the right balance between **repetition**, to hold the music together, and **variation** to prevent monotony.

This melody uses four notes per bar, but at only three different pitches, so that the 3-note group is on and off the beat on alternate repetitions:

➡ Select a clear, strong voice that sustains without dying away, such as a **solo synth**. Move to **Track 3** and set the sequencer for:
Track 3   **Midi Channel 4**   **Solo Synth**

➡ Set the tempo to 60 bpm and record the following melody.

Notes delayed until after the main beats are said to be played on the **off-beat.**

Moving notes ahead of the beat is known as **syncopation.**

Notice the syncopations in bars 2 and 4:

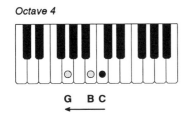

Octave 4

G   B C

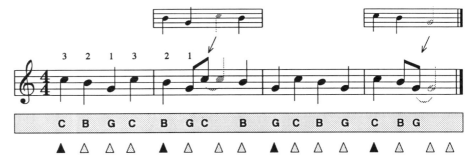

If you find it difficult to play the rhythm accurately, try recording the melody with even notes, as shown on the small staves above, and then move notes 7 and 15 two-sixteenths earlier on the grid.

➥ Look at the grid screen. Providing all of the notes are there and close to their right positions, quantize the track to *eighth-notes*. Don't quantize to quarters on this one, or you'll lose the syncopations.

After quantization the pattern should look something like this:

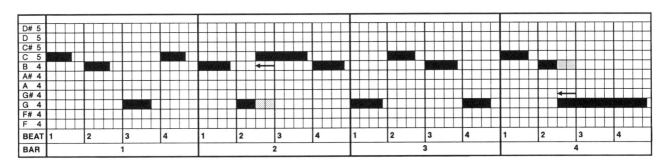

➥ Return the tempo to 120 bpm and switch off the metronome.

➥ Loop the track and listen back to all three tracks playing together.

Finally, before assembling the tracks into a complete piece, here is a simple suggestion for a rhythmic backing.

RHYTHM TRACK

➥ Select a voice with a dry, percussive quality, such as **block** or **xylophone**. Move to **Track 4** and record the following on:
Track 4   **Midi Channel 5**   **Block**

This, too, would be described as an off-beat pattern because it involves playing only on the weak beats of the bar (*ie* beats 2 and 4).

➥ Copy these two bars to make a four-bar pattern and save to disk.

Listen to all of the tracks playing together: the pattern probably sounds rather boring after a few loops. However, writing a brand-new pattern to follow on from this risks giving the effect of two different pieces sandwiched together.

The aim is to balance repetition and variation, so let's complete the piece by repeating the pattern, not by looping it but by *varying* it both in length and pitch: something the sequencer can do automatically.

Getting It Together

PATTERN COPYING

For *each* track (except the looped drum track, which does not need to be either copied or transposed) .....

➡ Copy bars 1–4 into bars 5–8 on the same track:

➡ Then create a half-length pattern by copying bars 7–8 into bars 9–10:

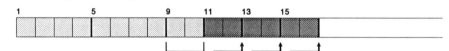

➡ Now copy this half pattern in bars 9–10 three more times, into bars 11–16:

TRANSPOSING

That is the repetition catered for. Finally, the variation. For this we again use **transposition** to shift some of the patterns to new pitches.

➡ Transpose bars 5–8 up five semitones, bars 11–12 up seven semitones, and bars 13–14 up five semitones on all tracks except drums:

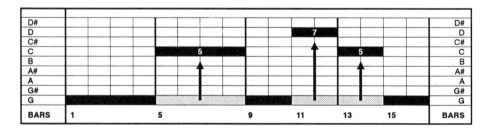

➡ Loop all of the tracks and listen back.

Make final decisions about the voicing for each track. You may need to balance the mix by adjusting track velocity levels – best done from the sequencer rather than changing the synthesizer set-up. In particular, make sure that the **kick drum** doesn't hide the bass part. Save your work to disk. As the piece doesn't have a definite stopping-point you may need to arrange a fade-out ending.

As with the first sequence, Sequence 2 was constructed with a minimal amount of original material. The score below outlines the full sixteen-bar piece:

Sequencing in patterns has avoided the need to play all but four bars of this piece. Obviously, much time can be saved if potential patterns in a piece of music are identified before recording starts.

Terms of Reference

The signs shown in this box are frequently used in notated music and will be found in many of the sequences in this book.

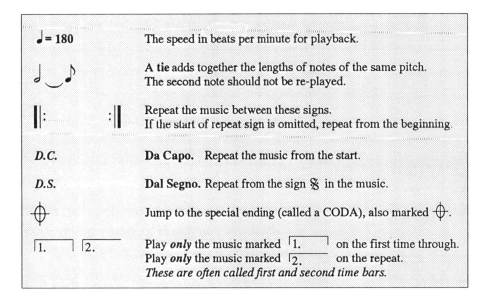

Developments

This new piece includes several copyable patterns and also uses the techniques of **syncopation** and **off-beat** playing encountered in Sequence 2.

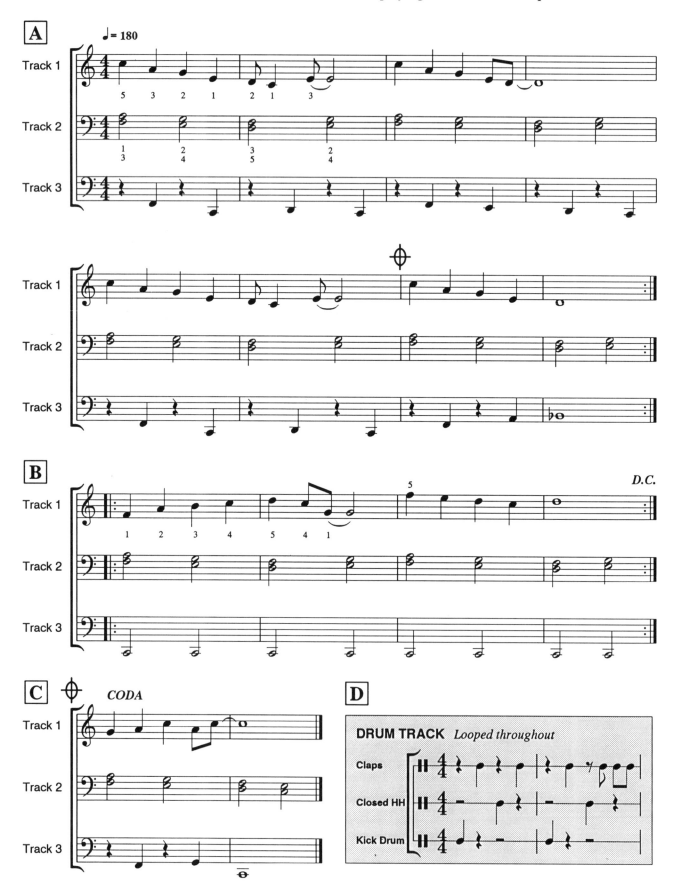

LAYOUT

Each track obviously needs to be recorded separately, probably at a slower tempo than the 180 bpm that would be ideal for final playback.

The melody on **Track 1** contains more than five different notes and so some fingering has been suggested to negotiate this problem. However, it can be seen that line one is almost the same as line two, and can be copied. Similarly, there are many copyable patterns to be found in **Tracks 2** and **3**.

The **repeat** marks indicate that the first eight bars (A) should be heard twice (*ie* copied), as should Section B.

Once these repeats have been made, the letters **D.C.** (*Da Capo*) indicate a return to the start of the piece for a third play-through of Section A. Normally this could be done by looping the tracks on the sequencer but, in this case, there is an alternative to bars 7 and 8 (Section C) to provide a clear ending (*Coda*). So, bars 1 - 6 need to be copied one more time, ready for this new material to be added at the end. No wonder so many song-writers take the easier option of a fade-out!

The following diagram may help to clarify the layout of the sequence once the various repeats have been made:

Bars	1-8		9-16		17-21	21-24	25-30	31-2
Tracks	A		A		B	B	A (bars 1-6)	C
Drums	D D D D		D D D D		D D D	D D	D D D	D

‖:   :‖

Music between **repeat** marks is played twice. A start of repeat mark *(left)* is often omitted if the music is to be repeated from the beginning. **D.C.** (**Da Capo**) is an additional way to indicate that the repeat is from the start.

VOICING

Decisions about voicing are vitally important, especially if the basic material is simple or repetitive. A good mix of voices can transform the effect of a sequence. Much more will be said about this in later chapters. Meanwhile, the following guidelines may be helpful:

Track 1: An **electric organ** or similar voice with a bright, crisp character. Repeated patterns could possibly be transposed up an octave.

Track 2: A sustaining electric voice. **A soft organ** sound may be suitable here.

Track 3: A very clear bass sound. Because it is written at low pitch anyway this need not be one of your synth's designated bass voices.

The funky style can be emphasised by keeping the melody notes very short, contrasting with the fully sustained chords on Track 2. You may feel that **electric drum** or **roto-tom** sounds on the drum track would be appropriate.

Sequence 3
Minimal Effort

Minimalism in music involves the use of very short patterns which are repeated and combined in various ways to give a sense of organic development. Although this sequence is 37 bars long, and uses seven different tracks, there are only thirteen bars of original material to be recorded. Most of the creative work is done by pasting these patterns into a musical collage over the continually repeated drum, bass and guitar parts. This chapter also introduces the concept of cycled recording, in which new material can be gradually added to a track which has been set to loop.

The Plan

Note-length quantization lets the musician adjust the endings of all the notes in a pattern. Most sequencers offer a variety of different types of note length adjustment.

To record a number of very short patterns onto separate tracks, where they can be quantized and edited before being copied and pasted into position to make a much more complex piece of music. The minimal amount of material and the need for complete rhythmic precision may make it simpler to input notes in step time for this sequence. The chapter also investigates the uses of note-length quantization to make the notes of certain patterns very short.

The Method

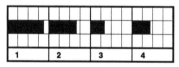

Notes after basic quantization

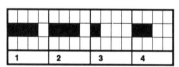

After note-length quantization to 16ths

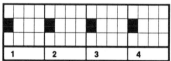

After fixed-length quantization to 16ths

The drum, bass and rhythm guitar tracks (A, B and C) form a constantly repeating backing known as an *ostinato* on which other patterns can be superimposed. The layout diagram on page 32 gives a possible arrangement of the material, although you will almost certainly be able to improve on this.

In addition to the basic quantization used in earlier sequences, rhythm-based music like this can often benefit from a **note-length quantize** to ensure that the *ends* of notes are regular *(see left)*. Sequencers also offer the option of a **fixed-length quantize** which makes all notes of the pattern the same length. Using a fixed-length quantize, all notes can be made very short *(staccato)* or can be expanded until there is no perceptible gap between them *(legato)*.

Only patterns G and H have any note-lengths that are not sixteenths, so fixed-length quantizing will definitely be an option for most tracks. The silence in the gaps between notes is as important as the sound of the notes themselves. When a note is shortened, the ensuing silence will inevitably be lengthened in order to preserve the correct start position of the next note.

PATTERN A

→ First, write the following two-bar drum pattern:

Claps															■	■	Claps
RotoTom								■									RotoTom
Cl. HiHat		■			■		■			■		■		■			Cl. HiHat
Kick Dr.	■		■		■		■	■		■		■		■		■	Kick Dr.
BEAT	1		2		3		4		1		2		3		4		**BEAT**
BAR				1									2				**BAR**

PATTERNS B-H

→ Record patterns B to H, *below,* onto seven suitably voiced tracks.

The dotted lines in the score separate the four beats of the single-bar patterns, while the grid further illustrates the precise rhythm and length of notes.

We used a deliberately distorted guitar voice for pattern C to contrast with the lead guitar pattern I, *overleaf.* The three trumpet tracks can share the same MIDI channel and voice number.

If you are step writing, you may have to create an empty one-bar pattern in the track before you can proceed.

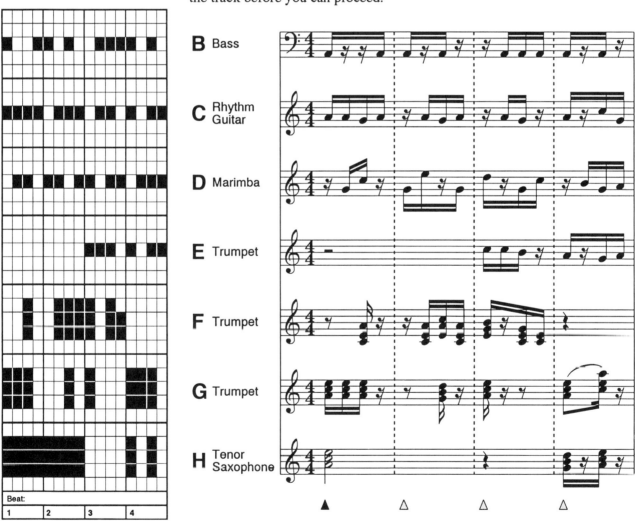

Patterns F, G and H contain chords which may prove tricky when recording in real time. Many sequencers have a **cycled recording** (or overdub) mode which allows recording into a pattern while it is looping, adding extra data on each pass. The chords could therefore be built up in layers, one note at a time.

PATTERN I

This pattern could be constructed by recording just the first bar and copying it three times. The few necessary pitch adjustments in bars 2, 3 and 4 can then be made on the grid – the sharp signs remain in force throughout each bar. If this pattern sounds too high for a guitar transpose it down one octave: guitar parts are traditionally written one octave higher than they are meant to sound.

I Lead Guitar

EDITING

You will need to quantize each pattern to sixteenth notes so that the starting points of notes are rhythmically precise (Pattern H could be quantized to eighth-notes, since none of its chords are as close as sixteenths).

It is essential that no pattern spills over its final barline, as this will make accurate copying impossible.

➡ Fixed-length quantize all patterns to make them sound *staccato* (try dotted thirty-seconds or even shorter lengths). This will also tidy up ragged bar endings. Manually re-lengthen the two longer chords in Patterns G and H.

ASSEMBLY

➡ Create the *ostinato* by copying and pasting the drum, bass and rhythm guitar patterns into the sequence as shown on the diagram *below*. Notice how the start points of these three tracks are staggered.

➡ Copy and insert the other patterns into the sequence at the points indicated, or in any other arrangement that sounds well. Try a playback speed of around 120 bpm.

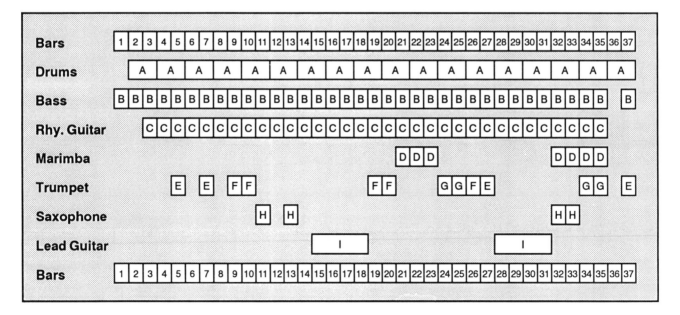

Final decisions can now be made about voicing and balance. Any changes in track velocity levels can be made from the sequencer.

➡ Listen to the mix at a fairly low volume to ensure that every element is clearly audible.

Recording engineers whose hearing has not been irreparably damaged by the high-level mixing of Heavy Metal often use this technique in the studio.

Developments

CHORDS AND SCALES

The effect of this sequence relies largely on the insistence and variety of its various rhythm patterns. This disguises the fact that the whole piece is based upon the notes of a single chord: A, C and E (with G and occasional other notes for interest). To reinforce this chord, the bass plays nothing but A throughout the sequence.

Most music uses a variety of different chords which form a harmonic structure for the piece. More on the uses and naming of chords in Sequence 4. Scale patterns are also very common. Even this one-chord piece contains fragments of scales, as in the falling contour of the Marimba part:

> A **scale** is a series of adjacent notes.

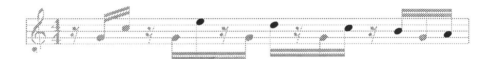

The Lead Guitar part similarly outlines a scale shape. You should be able to hear both of these clearly, as they are formed from the highest notes of their respective patterns. Each on its own does not radically disturb the overall effect of the underlying chord. You may have discovered, however, that these two patterns will not combine very comfortably – there are too many clashes when the different scales are superimposed.

Sequence 4
Working with Chords

Keyboard and guitar players will have noticed chord symbols printed above the melody line in much sheet music. These are indications of the harmony of the piece. Sometimes a song will, like the one opposite, use as few as three different chords, each based on a particular note of the scale. Deciding which scale, and therefore which chords, a piece uses can initially seem very confusing to the beginner. However, understanding how chords are built up and being able to use them effectively is vitally important for the musician. The basic concepts are explained below, although experimentation at the keyboard is by far the best tutor.

Scales and Keys

Most music is based on the notes of two types of pattern: scales and chords. A **scale** is a series of adjacent notes. The most common in Western music is the major scale, which you can find by playing the white notes from C up to the C an octave (eight notes) above. Although the keyboard is evenly spaced, you don't hear eight evenly spaced notes: the pattern of all major scales is:

Tone – Tone – Semitone – Tone – Tone – Tone – Semitone

This may not be obvious from the keyboard or from music notation, but your ears should spot the smaller semitone steps, and the sequencer's grid screen shows the pattern particularly clearly *(see left)*. It also demonstrates that if you start the scale on a different note, G for instance, you need some black notes (F# in this case) in the scale in order to maintain the pattern:

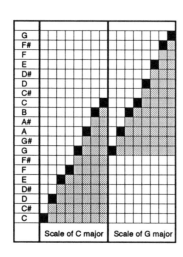

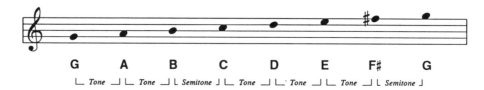

The set of notes that makes up a scale is known as a **key** (not to be confused with the key on a keyboard!). So, music that uses notes from the scale of G major is said to be in the key of G major and the music will use a **key signature** of F# *(see left)* to save writing this accidental before every note in the piece.

Easy Rider

The traditional blues song *below* is in the key of G major and uses F#.

➡ Record the melody, perhaps using a **saxophone** voice:

Ea - sy rid - er, see what you have done, Lord Lord, ____

Ea - sy ri - der, see what you have done, Ea - sy ri - der,

see what you have done, Ea - sy rid - er, Oh Lord.

PLAYING FROM CHORD SYMBOLS

The three chords in this song are based on notes one, four and five of a G major scale, as shown by the symbols **G**, **C** and **D**. A bass part is needed to provide a firm harmonic foundation and this can be derived from these chord symbols.

➡ Record 16 bars of bass track with the rhythm pattern shown *left* in every bar, but using the pitches G, C or D as dictated by the chord symbols. Each chord symbol remains in force until replaced by a new one.

MAJOR CHORDS

The concept of building basic 3-note chords (**triads**) is relatively simple. The bottom (**root**) of the chord is the note named in the chord symbol. The two higher notes are the alternate notes above this in the scale. A chord of **C** is formed by the notes C, E and G. Similarly, a chord of **G** comprises G, B and D. It is important to take into account the effect of any key-signature, so a chord of **D** consists of D, F# and A because the scale of G requires F *sharps:*

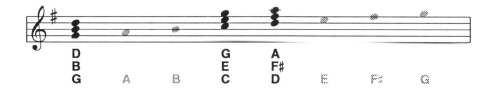

Chords do not always have to be played as close position triads like these. Any or all of the notes can be duplicated, allocated to different voices, spread over more than one octave (**open position**), have one of upper notes in the bass instead of the root (**inversion**), be split into patterns (**broken chords** and **arpeggios**), or be treated to any combination of these methods:

Chord of G

Close position   Open position   Inversions   Broken Chord   Arpeggio

➥ Create a guitar track from the chord symbols using open position triads. Try playing one chord on each quarter-note beat, as shown *left*. You may want to transpose this part up an octave.

➥ Similarly, record a smooth strings part, using triads in various inversions so there are no big jumps in pitch when the chord changes. Use long, sustained chords rather than separate triads in each bar, starting as follows:

There are literally thousands of ways of arranging the notes of even just three chords to make a backing for the song. Thinking quickly about different chords in their various positions is not easy, but familiarity will breed content!

Developments

MINOR CHORDS

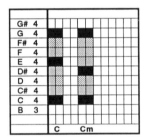

You will also encounter instructions in sheet music for other types of chord. The symbols **Cm** or **Dm** refer to **minor** chords. These are formed in exactly the same way as the major triads used in Sequence 4, except that the middle note of a minor triad is one semitone *lower* than in the major and the corresponding shape is different on the grid *(left)*.

The bass part does not always have to contain the root of the chord – sometimes having one of the other notes of the chord at the bottom of the texture will help the music to flow. In such cases, the chord is notated as **C/E** or **Gm/D** to indicate which note is to be played in the bass:

CHORD EXTENSIONS

A diet consisting only of simple chords can become somewhat dull – however, chords can be enlivened by adding notes to the basic triad. The addition of the 7th note above the root is the most common extension and the resulting "seventh" chord takes its name from the distance between its outer notes. This **interval** can be either major or, if lowered by a semitone, minor.

The symbol **C7** invariably refers to the lowered (minor) 7th, adding a B-**flat** to a C-major triad. **Cm7** also has a B-flat , but this time added to a C-minor chord. The **m** here refers to the *basic triad* being minor.

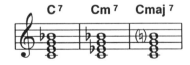

A C-major chord with added B-**natural** is notated as **Cmaj7** to distinguish it from the other forms of seventh chord. The **maj7** in this case refers to the *interval* and not the chord *(see left)*.

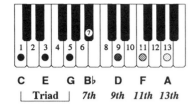

C E G B♭ D F A
| Triad | 7th 9th 11th 13th

Further alternate notes can be added on top of these seventh chords, producing ninths, elevenths and thirteenths:

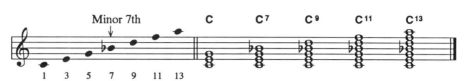

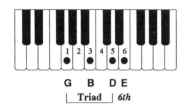

G B D E
| Triad | 6th

Another chord extension, very popular in jazz, is to add the interval of a sixth above the root of the basic triad. The presence of two adjacent notes (5 and 6) gives the chord a rich, slightly unfocused sound and causes the *added sixth* to be written slightly to one side in traditional notation:

SUSPENSIONS

Basic triads can also be changed by substituting one of their normal notes – generally the major or minor third. These are known as **suspensions** because, traditionally, the substituted note was left over (or *suspended*) from the previous chord. In many cases, the suspension is followed by the true note of the chord. Because a suspension changes the nature of the chord, it is notated in the chord symbols as **sus**.

PASSING NOTES

Passing notes are simply sections of scales that bridge the gaps between the notes of underlying chords. They occur constantly in all kinds of music, and form the essence of melody writing. They do not affect the chords themselves and are therefore not notated in the chord symbols, unlike suspensions. Passing notes (*) fall on weaker beats than the chords themselves – you will find examples of them in every sequence in this book.

WRITING CHORD PATTERNS

If you experiment long enough at the keyboard you will discover which chords sound well in sequence and which do not. There are many thousands of possible combinations, though, so the following guide-lines may be helpful.

The simplest plan is probably to use one chord per bar. They don't always have to be new chords, of course. If your song is going to have strong melodic and rhythmic content, you may find that the harmony could be more static, perhaps giving a pattern like this:

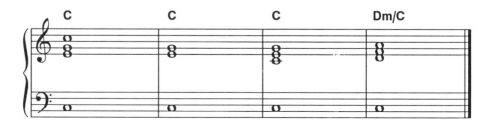

You may prefer to have more than one chord per bar, although too many chord changes can make playing difficult and the piece alarmingly hymn-like.

Certain chord patterns almost always sound effective – note the principles behind the following stock progressions, bearing in mind that it can be difficult to make a cliché sound fresh and original.

1. Chords falling down alternate notes of the scale: *eg* **C-Am-F-Dm**:

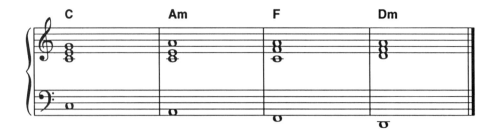

2. Chords moving to adjacent notes a tone apart: *eg* **C-Dm-Em** or **Am-G-F** (moving to an adjacent *semitone*, such as E-F, doesn't work nearly so well):

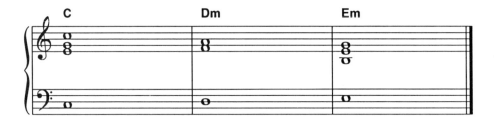

3. Chords whose lowest notes are four or five notes apart: *eg* **Am-Dm-G-C**:

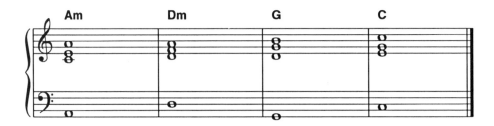

Chords sound best if the notes are not clustered around the bass, so in most cases the right hand will be required to play much of the chord. Generally, it is also better to avoid alpine contours in the right hand part by using inversions – particularly if the bass notes are also covering a wide range:

Sequence 5
Parallel Bars

Dealing with the harmonization of a single melody line or bass part encourages the musician to think vertically, working from the top down or from the bottom up, often for each individual note. Throughout history composers have also addressed the challenge of writing music which works horizontally, combining two, three or more melody lines simultaneously and allowing the harmony to occur from the juxtaposition of these themes. This process is known as **counterpoint**. *There are two options for contrapuntal writing – using different material which happens to combine successfully, or constructing a theme which will sound good against itself when using different starting points. This latter option is known as a* **canon** *or, in its simplest form, as a* **round** *such as the children's song, London's Burning.*

The Plan

To create a round by recording a seven-bar melody, copying it onto adjacent tracks and staggering their starting points. To explore the voicing techniques which will allow all parts to be clearly distinguishable while still blending attractively with each other in the overall texture.

The Method

The seven-bar melody, *overleaf,* works as a round. Notice that it begins with 3½ beats of recorded silence. The first note is played just before the start of a new bar: this is known as an **up-beat** start.

Remember also to play B-flats instead of B-naturals as indicated in the key-signature.

F-major uses B-flats
instead of B-naturals

You may find it easier to take the lower C with the left hand, since all of the other notes can easily be encompassed by the five fingers of the right hand. No sequencer yet on the market will be able to make much of the lyrics given here, but the authors thought you might like to sing-along with your sequence! (The advent of nearly affordable direct-to-disk recording, however, means that it is now possible to edit live tracks and vocals alongside a MIDI sequence).

When on   the train,   in   ca – ses of e – mer–gen –cy,   Pull down the chain, ___

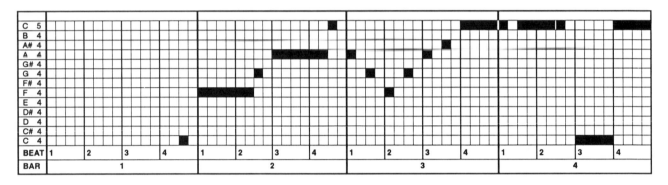

Pull down   the chain. ___   Pen – al – ty for im – prop – er use: Twenty five pounds.

Even if you record this melody at a very slow speed, you may find some of the rhythms difficult to play accurately in real-time against the metronome beat. If so, it might be easier to step-write the sequence. The finished grid, in either case, should look like the one below:

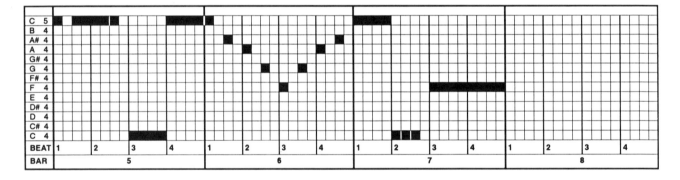

➥ Record the melody onto **Track 1** and quantize to the shortest note-value (here, sixteenth-notes). For counterpoint to work successfully really tight rhythm is essential.

➥ Make any other note-length adjustments which will help to clarify the rhythm. For example, although the traditional notation doesn't indicate any gaps between notes, all the eighth-notes will sound better if their lengths are shortened somewhat to let in some light, as shown on the grid: this is the technique known as *staccato*, explained on page 30.

➥ Copy the track twice more into bars 8–14 and 15–21 on the same track, save and listen back.

When on   the train, in

Music with an up-beat start like this is traditionally printed with an incomplete first bar, as shown *left,* and often an incomplete final bar as well. Most sequencers operate in terms of *complete* bars, so the technique used here of padding-out such incomplete bars with rests is often needed when sequencing.

There is no other music to record. The round is assembled by copying **Track1** onto the six adjacent tracks in such a way that the start of each new track is one bar later than the preceding one.

Most sequencers will allow material to be copied to a precise starting point on a new track. So **Track 2** should start at bar 2, **Track 3** at bar 3, and so on.

The alternative method would be to copy **Track 1** straight onto **Tracks 2 to 7** and then insert the relevant number of blank bars at the start of each track.

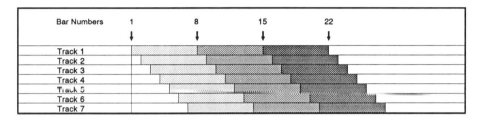

VOICING THE TRACKS

Because all of the parts in a round use identical material, it is particularly important to highlight each contrapuntal line by choosing distinctive voicing.

Here are three techniques to help achieve this:

1. Select seven voices with a clear, percussive attack. If you do not have a multi-timbral synth do not despair! In addition to the possibilities afforded by using a multi-track tape-recorder in conjunction with the sequencer, the two following suggestions can be used with any type of synthesizer.

2. Transpose some tracks to a higher or lower octave.

> **Offset** quantization will allow certain tracks or patterns to be moved fractionally off the beat. Some sequencers describe this as a plus or minus delay!

3. Offset certain tracks by advancing or delaying them a fraction to prevent them being masked by adjacent parts.

The later entries in the round are in particular danger of being obscured, so it might be worth making **Track 7** a bass part by transposing it down two octaves, which will also provide an effective ending to the round. **Tracks 4 to 6** would be the most likely candidates for offsetting or transposition up.

➡ Create a mix, select a suitable tempo and listen back.

Final decisions about voicing can only be made after the interaction between the seven voices has been heard. One "silly" voice somewhere in the texture can also be very effective.

Very few melodies will work as a round. This one succeeds because every strong beat consists only of notes from the chord of F-major. There are therefore no clashes in the harmony however many parts are playing together.

The round on the next page produces a far more complex chordal texture. This should be emphasized by using the same soft voice on all tracks.

Adieu, sweet Amaryllis

English 17th century

➡ Record this onto **Track 1** using a soft sustaining sound which will not decay on the long notes. The tempo marking of 120 bpm is an indication of the speed for playback. For recording it can obviously be much slower.

➡ Make sure that the notes all have their full length (*legato*) – the right hand fingering shown here makes *legato* playing possible without the need either to involve the left hand or, hopefully, to spend hours adjusting the note-lengths on the edit screen.

FINGERING

The easiest way to devise a workable fingering is to divide the music into sections (marked // here), the notes of which can all be played without having to move the hand. With the exception of the change of hand-position in bar 22 these shifts all take place where there is a beat's rest.

➡ Tidy up any non-*legato* playing by using a note-length quantize. The round sets up some chords which contain temporarily substituted notes (called **suspensions**). The *legato* style is needed to give these their full effect.

> **Velocity quantization** offers a means of adjusting the loudness of notes. It can be used to engineer a gradual increase or decrease in volume (*crescendo* or *diminuendo*). Whole tracks can be made relatively louder or softer or all notes can be set to the same velocity value.

It would also be a good idea to iron-out any startlingly loud or soft notes by adjusting their velocity to fit with their surroundings. A **set velocity quantize** would not be appropriate here as it would effectively obliterate all the slight changes in volume which make music expressive.

➡ Repeat the music by copying bars 2-25 into bars 26-49 of the same track. Then copy all of **Track 1** into **Tracks 2** and **3**, as shown *below*.

➡ In order to make a definite conclusion, cut both of these last two tracks so that they finish with **Track 1** at the end of bar 49:

Bar Numbers	1	9	17	26	33	41	50	
Track 1								
Track 2							DELETE	
Track 3							DELETE	

Sequence 6
Pachelbel's Canon

This canon by Johann Pachelbel is one of the undoubted masterpieces of the type of contrapuntal writing introduced in Sequence 5. It was originally written for three violins each playing identical material, staggered at 4-bar intervals. In the bass a 'cello or viola da gamba plays an ostinato pattern which forms the foundation of a simple chord sequence. The ostinato underpins a series of 27 variations created by the interplay of the upper parts. It was irresistible to include this work in a book about sequencing since it would be virtually impossible for a single player to perform it by any other means.

The canon is given here in full, in spite of the technical awkwardness of certain sections. Each repeat of the bass pattern, however, supports a perfectly self-sufficient variation so the faint-hearted can cut or end the sequence after any multiple of four bars, finishing with an appropriate C-major chord.

The Plan

To record the 113-bar melody in eight-bar patterns. Each one tends to use different note values which will make it imperative to edit and quantize every pattern separately. Also, to deal with various aspects of keyboard technique which arise in the process. To copy and stagger the theme onto two more tracks and add the ostinato bass.

The Ostinato Bass

➡ Record the following bass pattern onto **Track 1**:

These four bars should be copied 28 more times to provide a useful supplement to the metronome when recording the canon.

PATTERN ONE

➡ Record the first eight bars of the pattern onto **Track 2**. Choose a sustaining voice with a crisp attack. The four-bar rest at the start is for an initial play-through of the bass so the actual recording will need to start at bar 5:

➡ Quantize to half-notes and ensure that the note-lengths produce a *legato* effect without overlaps. Smooth-out any inconsistencies in velocity levels.

PATTERN TWO

Bars 13-21 use almost entirely quarter-notes:

➡ Record these eight bars making sure that the recording begins at bar 13. Try using a slightly slower tempo than was appropriate for Pattern One.

Some sequencers have a **Tempo Track** (Mastertrack) to control playback speeds. Ensure this is switched off while recording or it will continually over-ride individual tempo settings for each pattern whenever you listen back.

➡ Quantize to eighth-notes (anything longer would mean losing the final note of the pattern). Again, ensure that the notes are smooth and *legato*.

PATTERN THREE

These next eight bars will almost certainly require a slower tempo than previously used. Before recording, try marking-in some fingering which will produce a minimum number of hand-position changes. Lower notes could easily be played with the left hand in this section.

➡ Record, starting at bar 21.

➡ Edit where necessary, still preserving the *legato* style. It can be very effective to make **ascending** passages get gradually louder *(crescendo)* and descending ones softer *(diminuendo)*. Again, though, edit out any large velocity discrepancies between adjacent notes.

PATTERN FOUR   No big problems here!

➥ Record, starting at bar 29. It is important that the one-beat rests really do contain silence.

➥ Save and listen to the sequence so far.

If you are impatient to hear how the canon will sound when put together, copy the music so far recorded on **Track 2** into **Tracks 3** and **4**, starting these at bars 9 and 13 respectively. Play all four tracks together and make some preliminary decisions about voicing. The bass part, in particular, would be worth some attention at this stage.

PATTERN FIVE   This pattern, and a similar one later, illustrates very clearly that music which may be relatively simple to play on its original instrument can pose problems for the keyboard player.

It may appear at first to be too daunting even to attempt and could, if absolutely necessary, be left out completely, starting Pattern Six where Pattern Four finished. However, the option of recording at a very slow tempo or step-time writing makes it manageable even for the beginner.

➥ Record the pattern, trying not to press too firmly into the keyboard – only a few grams are actually needed to make the notes register. Notice how each bar has exactly the same rhythm. Quantize to sixteenth-notes.

➥ Try a **fixed length** quantize to make *all* notes one-sixteenth in length. In playing, the eighth notes would inevitably become shortened (*staccato*) and the process will emphasise this while providing a satisfying *legato* elsewhere.

➥ Save and take a break!

PATTERN SIX

➡ Record the following music into bars 45-52. Notice how the quarter-notes are on the off-beat in the second half:

➡ Try a note-length quantize to quarter-notes.

PATTERN SEVEN

This requires much the same treatment as Pattern Three. Again, lower notes can be taken with the left hand:

Legato playing is important in this example. The overall effect of this can be highlighted by making the first note in each group of four *staccato* to reflect the way a violinist would play it.

PATTERN EIGHT

These eight bars, from 61-68, make a feature of repeated notes:

This can be difficult to do on the keyboard, although the frequency with which it occurs in all kinds of music makes it a useful technique to learn. The secret is to keep the arm and wrist as relaxed as possible and not to try to play too firmly. Imagine that you are knocking on a horizontal door. The end result should be fairly *staccato*.

PATTERN NINE

This section is a slightly simpler version of Pattern Five. As earlier, the eighth-notes can be made *staccato* by fixed length quantizing to sixteenth-notes.

PATTERNS TEN – END

If you have managed to record up to here, the remainder of the canon should not present too many difficulties. Notice that the remaining number of 37 bars is not a multiple of the eight-bar pattern length which we have followed so far.

There are four more of these eight-bar patterns, but bars 101-104 seem to produce a single four-bar pattern. There is also, of course, the final bar which will ultimately produce the C-major chord for the ending.

> A **dot** after a note-value will increase its length by 50%. So a dotted eighth-note will last three-sixteenths of a beat. Note that the dot is worth half of the relevant note's length, and *not* necessarily half a beat.

➡ Record the rest of the sequence.

Try a fixed length quantize on the final eight-bar pattern (bars 105-112) to *dotted* eighth notes: this kind of figure often works better when played *semi-staccato*.

➡ Save and listen back to the entire canon with bass at about 110 bpm.

Final Mixdown

➥ Copy **Track 2** to **Tracks 3** and **4,** starting these on bars 9 and 13 respectively. If you already have parts of the canon on Tracks 3 and 4, these can safely be over-written.

➥ In order to achieve a tidy ending it will be necessary to delete all material after the first note of bar 113 on each of the four tracks. This final note should then be lengthened to fill the complete bar on every track.

➥ Engineer a gradual slowing-down of the tempo *(rit.)* in the penultimate bar (112) by reducing the speed for each beat by ten on the Tempo Track.

Gradual changes in speed are laboriously handled by most sequencers. Often it is necessary to alter the speed for each fraction of a beat in order to produce a convincing result.

➥ Voice the sequence – as the canon was originally written for three violins and bass it would be worth using the same voice for each melody track. Try a **pan flute** in preference to a synth string sound which, unlike their acoustic equivalents, often have too slow an attack *(see below).*

Evidence for pitch change has been found by comparing the length of organ pipes from instruments of the period with that of their modern-day counterparts.

The original canon was written in the key of D-major so the entire sequence should really be transposed up two semitones. However, this key was probably used in the first place because it gives violins access to more of their natural resonance than most other keys. This, clearly, is not applicable to the non-acoustic synth. In any case, pitch levels have risen by more than two semitones over the past 300 years, so our original recording key of C-major may well, in the end, prove to be more authentic.

Sound Shapes

Every sound has its own distinct character consisting of a unique pattern of waveforms which makes it distinguishable from any other. The information for reproducing these patterns is stored in the synthesizer, which is thus able to imitate any sound for which it has the data. More complex sounds require a greater amount of data in order to be reproduced successfully. This is why synths tend to sound less realistic with complicated acoustic sounds such as **live brass** or **strings**, than with electrically-originated sounds such as **digital organ** or **electric piano**.

Musicians wishing to find voices which combine successfully will particularly need to know the basic characteristics of the **envelope** for each sound. This is the term used to describe the profile which a voice creates, from the moment the key is pressed until after it is released and the sound has died away.

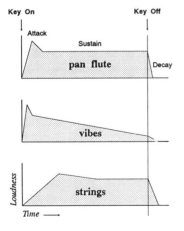

Try selecting three very different voices such as **pan flute**, **vibes** and **strings**. Notice how the attack of the first two is very immediate, although with **vibes** the sound initially decays very quickly. On the other hand, the **strings** sound seems to "bite" rather late. Plotted on a graph, these three sounds would look something like those shown *left.*

Developments

At the risk of this book seeming to become completely grounded in 300 year old counterpoint (don't worry!), here is a remarkable canon by Pachelbel's successor, the great J. S. Bach. More than any of his musical contemporaries, Bach was obsessed with the formal and mathematical implications of counterpoint. One of his finest achievements in this field was an increasingly complex series of canons and fugues (a more sophisticated contrapuntal form) known as *The Musical Offering*. The title arose because the work was dedicated to Frederick II of Prussia, who supplied the theme upon which the piece is based.

The Musical Offering is crammed with mathematical and musical games of all kinds – themes which work against themselves when inverted or reversed or have their note-values doubled. The permutations are endless.

This example is known, somewhat enigmatically, as the *Crab Canon:*

You may notice that the second part is actually the first part written backwards which, remarkably, provides the counterpoint. The second half of the canon is therefore an inverted mirror image of the first. This is the musical equivalent of a question which, when read backwards, provides its own answer and yet, when combined with itself, also gets up and makes the tea!

➡ Try recording onto two tracks using an appropriate keyboard voice of the period, such as **harpsichord** or **pipe organ.**

Some sequencers offer an option to perform a **retrograde** quantize which should allow you merely to copy **Track 1** and then reverse it. Remember, though, that note-*endings* will become note-*starts* under this process so a strict note-length quantize will be essential before starting.

Sequence 7
Music on the Air

Sequence 7 is a complete song in a somewhat more contemporary style! The funky bass part has a much more soloistic feel in this sequence, combining its previous function of underlining the chord patterns with that of acting as an important melodic and rhythmic line in its own right. The drum part is left to provide the fundamental beat, while the bass is mostly syncopated around it. You will notice that virtually every chord is one of the three types of seventh chord described in Sequence 4.

The Plan

The music for this sequence is printed over four continuous pages, in the format used by publishers of sheet music. There are three staves to each line of music, a vocal stave (for singing!) and an arrangement of the backing material on the pair of lower staves. Sheet music rarely has the space to include details of every nuance of the song. It relies on the purchaser being already familiar with the recorded arrangement.

The vocal line consists of a simple verse, largely on a **monotone** (single pitch), and a chorus that uses mostly mid-range notes. The verse could be spoken in rhythm, as a **rap**, but the chorus is better sung. The score also includes some indication of instrumental lines, allowing a breather for the singer. In the sequence, these can also double the vocal from time to time.

Reluctant vocalists may be relieved to find some suggestions later for making a purely instrumental arrangement – certainly a safer alternative than moving the synth to the bathroom in the search for flattering acoustics!

Even a song of this length is not so complex as it might appear. A little analysis (the *muso*'s favourite term for finding out how a piece was put together) shows that there are only a small number of different patterns. The following layout diagram "unpacks" the various repeat sections in the score (the signs used are explained on page 27) and shows how the backing consists of just three main patterns (A, B and C), each four bars long.

There is also an Introductory pattern (I) which returns at the end, in slightly different form, to make a frame for the song. A̲ indicates Pattern A with a new bass part while ↑ is a reminder that the chords pattern at this point needs to be transposed up an octave:

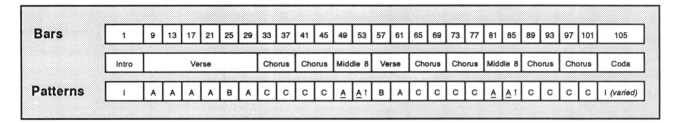

This layout diagram can be used as a template for copying patterns A, B and C in preference to recording every one of the 114 bars from scratch.

The Method

DRUM TRACK

Sheet music rarely gives away any details of the drum part – this is left to the imagination or aural memory of the player. For this song, it is more effective if the drums do not interrupt the sustained Introduction. Try step-writing this two-bar **fill** into bars 11 and 12, where it will create momentum for the start of the song proper and highlight the late entry of the main drum pattern:

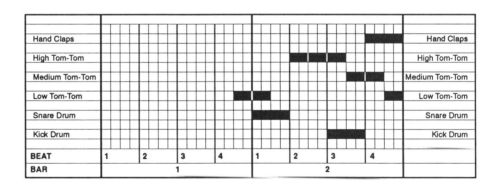

➡ Step-write the main drum pattern, *below*, into bars 13 and 14, and copy this two-bar pattern 45 more times to fill bars 13-104 of the song:

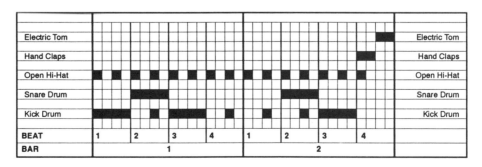

INTRO

These first eight bars consist of slowly rising seventh chords. The two staves in this section should be recorded onto different tracks so that they can be voiced separately (try **electric piano** for the chords and **synth bass** for the lower part). You may want to start softly and then add a *crescendo* for the last two bars. Remember to play B-flats, as indicated in the key signature.

The eighth-notes in the bass throughout this sequence need to sound *staccato* (nearer sixteenth-notes) as they would on bass guitar. The longer notes are more effective if given their full length.

Some sequencers allow you to quantize selectively, *eg* affecting only short note lengths. This could provide a simple means of transforming only the eighth-notes in this track.

VERSE AND CHORUS

➥ Record the main backing Patterns A (bars 9-12), B (25-28) and C (33-36), continuing on the two tracks used for the Intro. Make sure the chords in Pattern B are *staccato* to contrast with the *legato* style of the other two.

➥ Quantize to eighth-notes if necessary and make sure that all of the patterns are exactly four bars long, with no spillage into a fifth bar, before copying them into position, following the layout diagram on the previous page.

➥ Record the new bass part for Pattern A (bars 49-52) and insert copies at bars 53, 81 and 85.

When recording in gaps between other material, care is needed to avoid obliterating music in later bars. It may be easier to record on an empty track, checking for exact length before inserting into the body of the song.

Alternatively, most sequencers have a **Punch-In** (or Replace) facility for adding new material in the middle of a track without erasing the music on either side. This is done by setting a precise bar location for both the beginning and end of the recording. Unlike **overdubbing**, which allows new material to be superimposed on the original, punch-in replaces the old take.

➥ Transpose the piano track up an octave in bars 53-56 and 85-88.

CODA

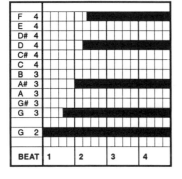

The music from bar 105 to the end repeats the Intro, with an added ending. However, the wavy line before each chord indicates that the notes should be spread like a slowly strummed guitar chord. Notes of a chord played consecutively rather than simultaneously are known as an **arpeggio**.

In this case, the distance between the note entries should gradually decrease as you get towards the top of the arpeggio, so as to sound improvised *(see left)*. It will probably be easiest to copy the intro and then shift the notes on the grid.

Notice the tempo change to 90 bpm. Bar 113 is an attempt to show a sustained arpeggio in notation. All notes in this bar should be played on the piano track, the bass simply holding an eight-beat D.

CHORUS

Even with a sung vocal, the song needs a couple of extra instrumental voices, particularly in the chorus sections.

➡ Record the vocal line of the chorus (bars 33-40), adding the bar-long D which overlaps with the repeat (bar 41). Voice it for **guitar.**

➡ Copy this nine-bar pattern onto a fresh track for the repeat, starting at bar 41. Voice for **brass** and transpose up an octave if necessary.

These patterns can also be used for the other chorus sections (bars 65-80 and 89-104). However, if you are performing the song with live vocals, you will need to use the revised melody given for the last chorus.

The brass will also be useful in playing the unexpected sustained D in bars 112-113, which does not form part of the piano track.

MIDDLE EIGHT

There is an eight-bar instrumental solo printed on the vocal stave at bar 49

➡ Record this on **trumpet**, making the short notes very *staccato*. Then copy to the corresponding point (bar 81) in the *Dal Segno* repeat. The first four bars of this solo also appear in bars 61-64.

INSTRUMENTAL VERSION

The effect of the vocal part in the verse depends upon the words and is too repetitive merely to be assigned to an instrument if you are not using a singer. However, the trumpet can be used to *outline* some of the music, as follows:

➡ Record, starting at bar 14, and then repeat in the next four bars, transposed up an octave. Notice the two and a half beats rest at the start of the pattern. The transposed pattern can also be used again, starting at bar 28.

The vocal line in the coda might also be covered by the trumpet in an instrumental version, although it will need careful velocity quantizing. To match the dreamy effect that a singer would create here, you might feel like playing this part in freehand (without metronome) so that it doesn't sound tediously regular.

Developments

A strong bass line is necessary to act as a foundation for chord structures; in many kinds of music it also supplies as much rhythmic energy as the drums. Frequent syncopation and wide leaps between notes, as in the bass of the third extract *overleaf,* are a natural part of bass guitar playing – difficult to do on the keyboard, but important if bass parts are to sound convincing.

The fragments *below* feature some suggestions for bass lines. They are intentionally incomplete – use them as starting points for new songs:

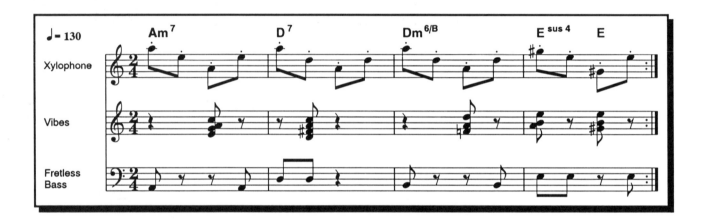

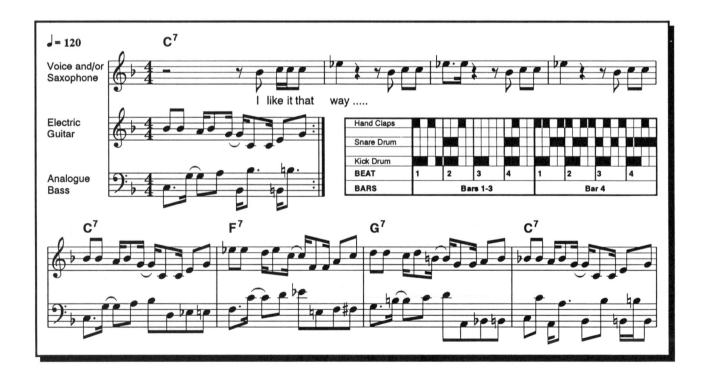

Sequence 8
Gershwin's *"Lady, Be Good"*

Since his untimely death in 1937 of a brain tumour, George Gershwin has gradually gained recognition as one of the most influential composers in American musical history. Songs such as "Summertime", "Swanee" and "I Got Rhythm" have justly become popular standards, whilst his "cross-over" works for the concert hall – "An American In Paris" and "Rhapsody In Blue" – made a tremendous impact on the conservative audiences of the time. The importance of his jazz-opera "Porgy and Bess" is only now beginning to be fully realised. "Lady, Be Good" was written by George and his brother, Ira Gershwin, for their first Broadway musical in 1924. The lyric is given here for karaoke *enthusiasts.*

The Plan

Like most popular songs of the time, "Lady, Be Good" contains only a limited amount of original music, with its two contrasting eight-bar sections arranged into an A-A-B-A structure. All of this material is notated overleaf in full score, each line forming a different track. The sequence makes a feature of swing rhythms, in which some beats are divided into threes, creating **triplet** patterns.

The Method

➡ Arrange the first 16 bars of the song by recording the eight bars (A) given for each track, and repeating them. Use the **first time** bars for the initial play through but replace them with the **second time** bars on the repeat as these are different on the trumpet, marimba and bass tracks.

TRIPLET RHYTHMS

Notice that many beats in the drum parts are divided into three rather than the two or four used in earlier sequences. This produces a note-length known as a **triplet** eighth-note giving a swing effect.

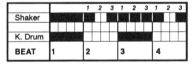

Traditional notation unhelpfully prints these shorter notes to look exactly like eighth-notes, with only a figure *3* on each affected beat to show this triple sub-division. Once again, the sequencer's grid screen provides a much clearer picture of what is actually going on in, for example, bar 4 *(see left)*.

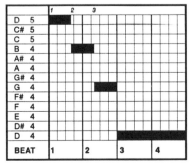

In order to step write this drum pattern you will need a resolution which divides each beat into triplets when entering notes (*eg* 8T for eighth-note triplets).

Notice also that bars 3 and 5 of the guitar track contain triplet *quarter*-notes. This means fitting three notes of equal length into the space of two beats. The mathematically minded will realise that the second note has to come *before* the second beat and the third just *after* it *(see left)*. Mousing them into position on the grid, using a 4T triplet resolution, is probably the simplest option.

SECTION A

This song needs a relaxed feel to the rhythm. Ruthless quantization could easily be counter-productive, making the piece sound square and boring.

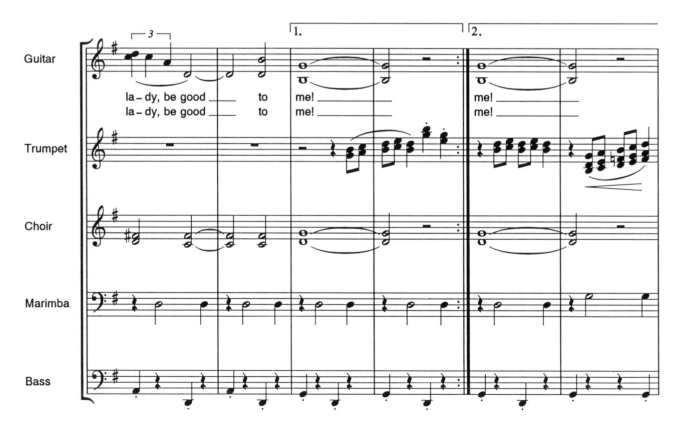

See the Terms of Reference box on page 63 for an explanation of the various new musical signs used in this sequence.

Indications of voicing are only suggestions – the final mix will depend largely on your synth's own resources. Some tracks may need to be transposed up or down an octave to sound effective. The four-bar drum pattern can be copied as it is (or varied, if you are feeling creative) for use throughout the song.

SECTION B

The following section, known as the **Middle Eight**, is played in bars 17-24, after the repeat of the first section (remember to use F-sharps):

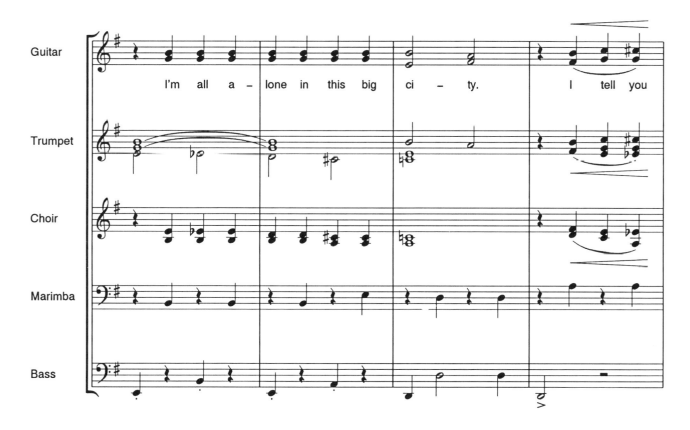

In the Middle Eight the trumpet and marimba briefly echo the swing effect of the triplet eighth-notes used in the drum part. If you want to get the feel of this, imagine Frank Sinatra singing "doo-bee-doo-bee-doo".

SECTION A (varied)

The final section is much the same as the first, but there are enough differences to make it worth recording most tracks afresh. This has the advantage of not sounding like yet another carbon copy: a hazard of repetitive sequencing.

The trumpets here have more triplet eighth-notes, as well as imitating the triplet quarter-notes in the guitar part. The trumpet sound needs to be particularly gentle, almost thin. This may require voice editing on the synth to reduce the attack level and intensity: check your manual.

➡ Record and insert this final section into bars 25-32.

➡ Copy the entire song for a complete repeat and create a final mix.

Although many cover versions of "Lady, Be Good" take a fairly brisk upbeat tempo, Gershwin's original marking is **slow and gracefully**. Try a tempo of around 110 bpm.

Developments

COMPOUND TIME-SIGNATURES

In music with frequent triplet patterns it is often easier to use a time-signature which indicates that *all* beats are divided into threes, to save writing the figure *3* over every sub-divided beat The beat itself, in such cases, is written as a dotted quarter-note (*ie* 3 eighth-notes). In spite of the differences in notation, the following two immensely useful patterns will sound exactly the same:

The equivalent compound time-signature for $\frac{4}{4}$ is $\frac{12}{8}$.

The time-signature $\frac{9}{8}$ indicates a triplet version of $\frac{3}{4}$ time.

Terms of Reference

C	An alternative version of the $\frac{4}{4}$ time-signature.
♩ ♪	Dots indicating that notes should be played *staccato*.
⌒	Phrase marks show that groups of notes should be played *legato*.
♫ (3)	Three triplet eighth-notes (= one quarter-note in total length).
♩ ♩ ♩ (3)	Three triplet quarter-notes (= one half-note in total length).
f mf p	Abbreviations of the Italian words for loud, medium loud and soft.
< >	*Crescendo* and *diminuendo* marks (hairpins).
♩ ♪ (>)	Notes with accents are played louder than others.
$\frac{6}{8}$ $\frac{9}{8}$ $\frac{12}{8}$	Compound time-signatures for 2, 3 and 4-beat bars.

Sequence 9
And Now For Something Completely Different .....

*Devotees will already be familiar with Sequence 9 as the signature tune to "Monty Python's Flying Circus". It first appeared in 1893 as a march for military band by Sousa, called **The Liberty Bell**. There exists a huge repertory of band music, particularly from the latter half of the nineteenth century, in the days before motorised combat. Bands today consist of up to sixty wind and brass instruments, ranging in pitch from piccolo to tuba, plus the ubiquitous bass drums, cymbals and side drums. Marches are characterised by their unswerving adherence to a strict beat which makes them ideal sequencing material. **The Liberty Bell** is in compound time, and therefore each basic beat consists of three eighth-notes, rather than the more usual two.*

The Plan

To record the five basic tracks shown *opposite*. In order to imitate the thick, rich texture of an authentic band it will then be necessary to copy and transpose certain tracks up or down an octave and assign them different voices. To provide even more variety it is possible to make voice changes during the course of the track. Finally, to explore the use of drum rolls and certain ornaments such as grace notes and trills.

The Method

DRUM TRACK

➡ Write the drum part first. It will be far more musical than the metronome beat when recording other parts, and will help to keep them "in step".

➡ Remember to set the time-signature to 6/8. This may have to be done on the Mastertrack on some sequencers. You do not have to use triplet grid resolution for step-writing in compound time.

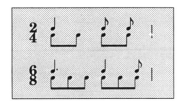

Compound time-signatures can often provide pitfalls for the first-time user. The most important thing to remember is that although music in 6/8 has two beats per bar, every beat is *three* eighth-notes in length. Each one-beat note will thus be notated as a *dotted* quarter-note and the grid *(see opposite)* will look markedly different from a 2/4 or 4/4 grid. A normal quarter-note will only last for two-thirds of a beat in this time-signature.

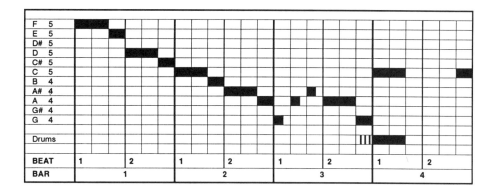

The three small notes in the side drum part are known by drummers as a **drag**, and should be played as three thirty-second notes immediately *before* the beat, even though the notation seems to suggest that they occur after the bar-line.

Notes with three beams across their stems ♪ indicate a **tremolo**, which means that the note length should be split into repeated thirty-second notes.

INSTRUMENTAL TRACKS

➡ Notice the key-signature of B-flat for the instrumental parts. This changes to B-flat and E-flat for Section C.

The ♪ which occurs occasionally in Track 1 is known as a **grace note**, and is played as a thirty-second note immediately before the beat. Don't put these in until *after* quantization to eighth-notes or they will be crushed onto the beat.

Notice that in the Intro *(below)*, Tracks 2, 3 and 4 can be copied and transposed from Track 1. Section C on page 68 is repeated, but only the first 12 bars can be copied as there is a different four-bar ending on the second time through. The drum track is less repetitive than in many a pop song, but there are still plenty of opportunities for copying patterns. It is well worth sequencing the full part given, as substituting a drum machine pattern (even if you can find one in 6/8 time) will lose much of the military character.

INTRO

SECTION A

SECTION B

SECTION C

Mixdown

ASSEMBLY

➡ Check that all four melody tracks are tightly quantized, and that note-lengths are precise. The latter is particularly important where all tracks end simultaneously (*eg* bar 4 of the Intro). Set the tempo to 160-176 bpm.

➡ Make sure that the contrast in dynamics (velocity levels) between Sections A and B is effective and that the various dynamic markings in Section C are clear. You can make velocity changes for all tracks at once on many sequencers if the actual playing levels for each track are wide of the mark.

> The Italian word **Fine** at the end of Section B means that the *Da Capo* repeat must end here.

➡ Copy the first 12 bars of Section C for the repeat and add the second-time ending *(above)*. Finally, copy the Intro, and Sections A and B to the end of the sequence, as indicated by the letters **D.C.** (*Da Capo* – repeat from the start). The complete layout should look like this:

Bars	1-4	5-20	21-36	37-52	53-68	69-72	73-88	89-104
Sections	Intro	A	B	C 1	C 2	Intro	A	B

ORCHESTRATION

To sound authentic this piece clearly needs a selection of brass and reed voices, including trumpet and saxophone. You will probably feel that the bass part needs re-inforcing, in which case copy Track 4 onto a spare track and transpose it up an octave. This new part can use either the same or an extra bass voice.

In a live band performance the melody (Track 1) would be played by trumpets or cornets, doubled by other instruments. Try copying the entire part onto a fresh track and assign it a new MIDI channel. This new track can then be transposed, and voiced from the sequencer using MIDI, as explained *overleaf.*

PROGRAM CHANGING

In addition to actual notes, sequencer tracks can contain other MIDI data, used for controlling events such as program (voice) changes, pitch bend, sustain pedal and aftertouch. A program change message will enable you to change to another voice in the middle of a track without altering the MIDI channel. Different sequencers, however, use varying methods for inputting and displaying this MIDI information. Generally, the value placed in a program change command will be the same as the new voice number on your synth. Check your sequencer manual for details of all of this.

Here is a suggestion, using program changes, that uses the extra melody line copied from Track 1 to give more of the flavour of an American band:

➡ Transpose the first 20 bars of this new track up two octaves and voice it for **flute**. This will sound like a piccolo at this pitch.

➡ Transpose Section B down an octave and add a program change to **low brass** to give a trombone effect.

➡ Transpose the rest of the track up two octaves, adding a program change to **glockenspiel** (or **vibes**) for the repeated Section C. Return to **flute** for the remainder of the piece.

There are endless possibilities for arrangement using the material in any of the tracks. The only limit is the time at your disposal!

Developments

There is one final piece of ornamentation which will enhance the portions of the new track voiced for flute. In band music, the agility of the piccolo is often used to add brilliance to the ensemble by trilling on long notes.

A **trill** is a succession of very fast notes (thirty-second notes will do at this tempo). These alternate between the written note and the next note up in the scale.

➡ Add a trill to the long D in bar 8 of the flute track by replacing it with D and E alternately in thirty-second notes:

Don't forget that transposition will cause the music *above* to sound two octaves higher than written at this point. Trills can also added to the long notes in bars 12 and 16 of the same track. Copy all three sets of trills into the corresponding bars in the repeat of this section (bars 76, 80 and 84).

Sequence 10
Psyclone

*Sequences 10 and 11 show how two features of the Sousa march, compound time and grace notes, also appear in contemporary song-writing. **Psyclone** is in compound time but, unlike Sequence 9, it has a very laid back feel to it. The guitar track provides an opportunity to experiment with keyboard **aftertouch**. It also explores the rhythmic tensions created when a melody that does not conform to the dotted quarter-note beat coincides with the standard backing.*

The Plan

To save showing unnecessary repeats, all the backing music for each of the four sections has just been printed once. The various patterns for each track can then be copied or deleted as shown below. The arrows identify patterns which will need to be transposed up an octave. The vocal part on page 74 can either be sung along with the completed sequence or it can be plundered to provide material for an additional instrumental track.

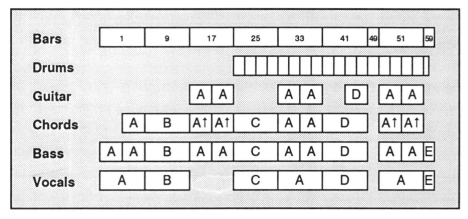

The diagram shows the structure of the song, with a repeating **chorus** (A) and contrasting **middle eights** (B, C and D). Notice how the drum solo in bars 49-50 prevents the 8-bar structure becoming too predictable.

The backing music for this song has been notated in a key which is easy to read, but is too high for singing without using steroids! After the sequence has been completed, transpose bars 1-31 down five semitones and bars 32-61 down four semitones for all tracks (except the drums). The vocal part has already been transposed to these new keys.

The Method

The bass can be *staccato* throughout the sequence (perhaps using a fixed-length quantize to eighth-notes on all but the longest notes). Use a dry voice, such as **pick bass**. The chords, however, need the precise lengths shown in the score. **Vibes** would be suitable here, perhaps changing to **strings** for Pattern D.

PATTERN A

PATTERN B

PATTERN C

DRUM PATTERN

The drum track starts at bar 25. It will need to finish at the end of bar 59:

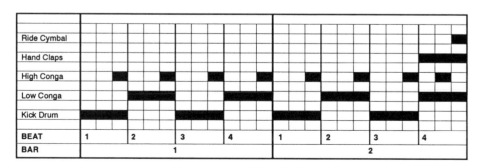

PATTERN D

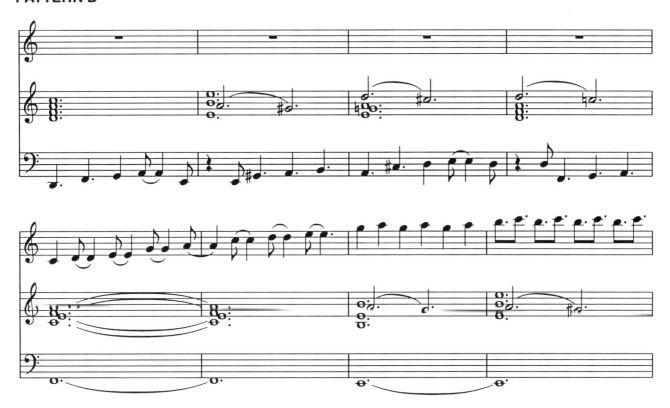

Patterns B and C do not contain a guitar part. The grid *below* may help clarify the rhythm of the guitar part when it returns in the second half of Pattern D:

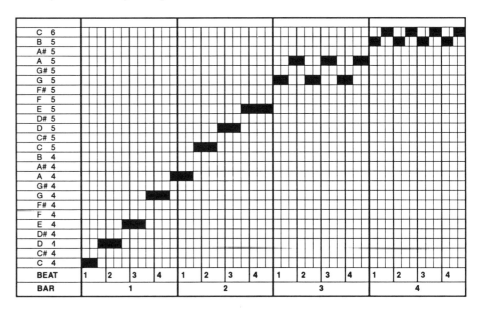

AFTERTOUCH

Many keyboards will respond to further pressure after the note has started. This **aftertouch** can be used to change parameters, such as tone colour and pitch. Most guitar voices are programmed to add *vibrato* if aftertouch is used. Try it on the long notes in the guitar track, *eg* Pattern A, bars 1 and 3.

PATTERN E

Pattern E *(left)* contains a note which is off the keyboard of many synths and will have to be accessed by transposition or be step-written. MIDI offers 127 note numbers and most instruments will respond well beyond the range of their keyboards, providing at least seven octaves on many voices.

VOCALS

The vocals for *Psyclone* are already at the correct pitch for singing with the transposed sequence. They contain interesting cross-rhythms where bars of six quarter-notes are superimposed on the 12/8 bass part. Much of the vocal could be adapted as an instrumental track, particularly the *scat* section at the end, although the sequence should also sound satisfactory without any of this part. If you do use a singer, you may prefer to add an extra four bars of Pattern A at the start to act as a lead-in and to set the pitch for the vocals.

Sequence 11
Cast Your Net

This song appears more complex in structure than **Psyclone.** *In fact, a single four-bar riff (Pattern A) serves as backing for much of the verse as well as for the chorus. Variety is provided by a number of trumpet fills and changes in texture. The vocal music on page 78 plays a much more important rôle in this sequence and ways of incorporating it on instrumental tracks will be explored later on. Firstly, though, the backing tracks can be assembled as shown below. The upward arrows indicate patterns which need to be transposed up an octave:*

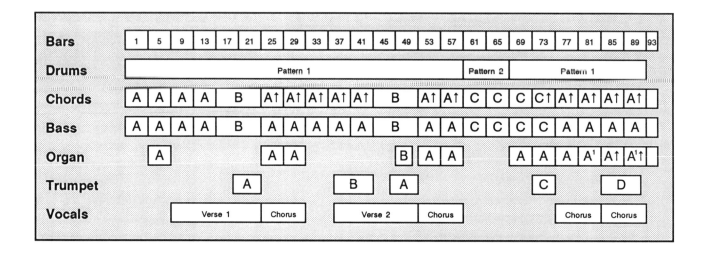

DRUMS

Pattern 2 is two bars long and appears only four times, in bars 61-68. Pattern 1 can be used for the rest of the song:

CHORDS AND BASS

These two tracks are made up of three patterns (A, B and C) plus a chord to provide an ending. As so often, the bass part needs to be *staccato* everywhere except on the longer notes in Pattern C *(opposite)*. Try **brass** and **dry bass** voices for the two tracks:

PATTERN A

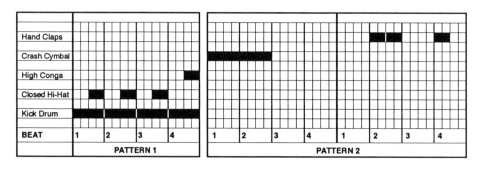

PATTERN B

PATTERN C

ORGAN

Grace notes are often used by pianists when a blues feel is required. The blues scale includes several slightly flat notes which are not accessible with the fixed pitch of a keyboard. Grace notes deceive the listener into thinking that the main note is flatter than it actually is. Here they should be played as thirty-second notes *before* the beat and, as in Sequence 9, they will probably have to be put in after quantization to avoid them being shifted.

The quarter-note triplets *(right)* replace the last bar of this pattern in bars 84 and 92 only:

Pattern B has not been printed because it simply doubles the bass track in bars 49-51. It can be copied across but will need to be transposed up three octaves. A bright **electric organ** voice with fast attack is needed throughout this track.

ENDING

This final chord *(left)* is needed in bars 93-94 on all three backing tracks. Try a program change on the chords track to something stratospheric for these last two bars. Synthesizer programmers back at the factory usually include a few truly weird options in the upper reaches of the voice list. They are seldom of any use, except for frightening people. This is one of the few exceptions!

Live bands distribute their sound sources around the stage, creating a three-dimensional aural picture. This effect can be reproduced on most multi-timbral synths by **panning** sounds to the left and right of the stereophonic spectrum. This will create "space" in the centre of the mix for the vocals.

VOCALS

The notation in the vocals is a compromise between the short note-lengths you would need to make the part sound good as an instrumental track, and the smoother, more *legato* style used by most singers. Notation can only ever be a guide to performance. The part as written will sound quite reasonable on **sax**, but remember that many of the repeated notes (*eg* bars 18-20) are tied to the lyrics; on an instrumental track they can be joined together or even carry a different rhythm entirely. You need only follow the basic melodic shape. Try experimenting with this, particularly if you are not planning to sing the vocals.

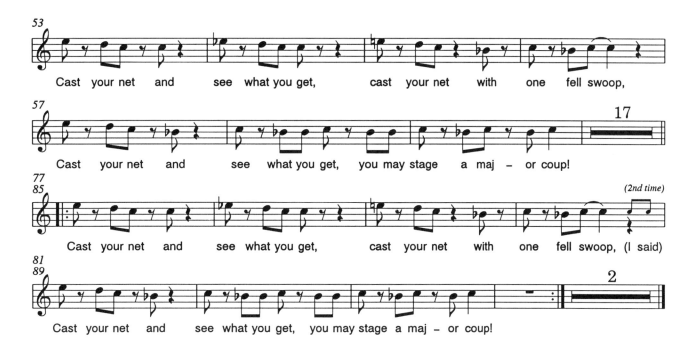

Cast your net and see what you get, cast your net with one fell swoop,

Cast your net and see what you get, you may stage a maj – or coup!

Cast your net and see what you get, cast your net with one fell swoop, (I said)

Cast your net and see what you get, you may stage a maj – or coup!

TRUMPET

The four fills *below* will give extra rhythmic impetus to the song, especially on the run-up to each chorus. **Muted trumpet** would sound good on this track. Pattern A "shadows" the vocal part in bars 21-24 — the main outline is there, although some of the rhythms are different. These trumpets fills, and pattern D in particular, should sound very *staccato*.

FINAL MIXDOWN

There are a couple of techniques which can be used to generate extra energy. Firstly, set a *crescendo* from bars 69 to 85. This can start quieter than the preceding material. Set velocities as high as you dare for the last ten bars. You can also marginally increase the tempo at bar 69 and again at bar 73 where the trumpet comes in. However, you will find that once the last chorus has started, any further increase in speed will just sound manic.

Transpose the whole song into a key comfortable for singing. Music often seems to sound better in some keys than others. Our own experiments found that this song will sound good 1 or 3 semitones higher (or 4 semitones lower), but less successful in other keys.

Sequence 12
Baroque Formations

*The two works in this chapter show different aspects of music by J. S. Bach. His obsession with counterpoint has already been mentioned in Sequence 6, and these pieces also feature short, repeated rhythm patterns which act as motors for the music in the absence of a drum kit. Synthesized Bach is by no means a new concept – the springy bass parts and clarity of texture, combined with an absolutely regular tempo, make much of Bach's music ideal for sequencing. The extract overleaf is from **Cantata 51** for Soprano, Trumpet and Strings; the piece below is a **Gavotte** from one of Bach's many sets of dance music for keyboard.*

Gavotte from the French Suite in G

Bach rarely included indications of speed, dynamics or phrasing in his scores, and so these aspects are left to the performer. Using creative voicing or even adding drum parts will not detract from the immense stylishness of this music. Bach was a great arranger of both his own and other people's work and it is interesting to speculate on the uses he would have made of MIDI technology.

What will kill this music stone dead, however, are stodgy textures and the sort of ponderous, rhythmically slack performances which used to be all too common and which did Bach no favours at all.

PHRASING AND ARTICULATION

The Gavotte is a fairly quick dance with just two half-note beats per bar, as shown by the ¢ time signature. All quarter-notes in the bass part will probably sound best if shortened to eighth-notes. The springy effect can be further accentuated by similarly shortening quarter-notes in other parts, wherever they occur in the second half of the bar (*eg* the first two notes of the piece). Eighth-notes can probably be left *legato,* but bear in mind that all these points are only suggestions and experimenting will be important here.

Baroque music tends to use only basic dynamic contrasts between loud and soft. Devices such as *crescendo* or *diminuendo* will sound out of place, but try contrasting velocities for the repeats. Notes on the first beat of each bar may well be slightly louder than others, providing energy for the dance.

Aria from Cantata 51

In this piece, two solo parts (originally trumpet and voice) are backed by a string orchestra. Traditionally they are also joined by a keyboard player (organ or harpsichord) who would improvise a part combining the written bass line with appropriate chords and melodic fragments. A simple means of producing this *continuo* part will be suggested later on.

Notice how the first notes on adjacent beats often form scales of their own (*eg* bars 6-7 in the Violin 1 part). The velocities of these notes can be boosted fractionally to highlight them in the texture. Record on clear, "immediate" voices – many synth string voices will speak too slowly for this kind of music. There is, of course, no need to imitate orchestral sounds at all: a completely electronic voicing may well work better.

The trumpet trill in bars 6-8 can be written as thirty-second notes, starting on the note above (A) and continuing for ten and a quarter beats.

All eighth-notes can be somewhat *staccato* to give rhythmic bounce – the exception might be the soprano part where a live singer would inevitably sound more *legato* than either trumpet or strings. This part is not needed for the repeat, which ends after the first beat of bar 9. You will need to engineer a slight slowing-up for the last few beats.

CONTINUO

An acceptable keyboard part can be made by creating a fresh track and **merging** the MIDI data from the lowest three tracks onto it. Most sequencers offer this facility, but take care to get the source and destination tracks the right way round. This merged track will almost certainly need reduction in volume – a continuo part is only an accompaniment. Voice for **organ** or **harpsichord**.

The orchestra would also contain a double bass, playing the 'cello part transposed down an octave. Creating a track for this will help to balance the relatively high pitch of the upper parts.

Sequence 13
Flying Solo

Producing solo lines which sound both realistic and spontaneous is one of the major challenges facing the synth user. Techniques which come naturally to, say, a saxophone player, such as squeezing the pitch or changing the tone colour of notes, can be very difficult to reproduce successfully on the keyboard. MIDI offers a number of features to help overcome this problem. The first piece in this chapter aims to show how, by using pitch bend, modulation, aftertouch and other controllers, an otherwise obviously synthesised sax solo can be made to sound more like the real thing.

MIDI Controllers

We have already heard how the sound of a note can be modified from the keys, by using aftertouch. Synths have a range of other facilities for adapting the character of a voice, going under the general heading of **controllers**.

These controllers include a volume pedal, a sustain pedal (to prolong the sound after the fingers leave the keys) and wheels (or a joystick) for modulation and pitch bend. Some manufacturers even provide a breath controller which utilizes the player's breathing to simulate the attack of a live wind instrument, ensuring that hardly any part of the anatomy is unoccupied. A few synths include this controller as part of a multi-function joystick.

Most synths allow the controllers to be programmed by the user. One useful technique for live players is to assign program changes to a foot pedal, thus allowing voices to be altered without the hands leaving the keyboard.

Playing with one hand on a control wheel or joystick means that many of the effects are only possible or, indeed, suitable for playing solo melodic lines. **Pitch bend**, for example, will flatten or sharpen the sounding pitch of a note, like a blues singer or guitarist "bending" a note. **Modulation** most commonly produces a slight fluctuation in pitch, warming the sound like the *vibrato* of a string player. **Breath control** gives a pulsing of intensity, similar to the natural *tremolo* of a wind player.

The information produced by controllers is as much a part of MIDI data as are the pitch and velocity of notes. It can thus be recorded or step written on a sequencer. In very complex sequences an excessive amount of controller information on many channels simultaneously can choke the MIDI system, causing timing problems in the music. As controller data is both bulky and often not needed, both synths and sequencers generally have filters to prevent it being transmitted or received. Check that any such MIDI filters are not operating for this chapter.

PITCH BEND

The most common uses of pitch bend involve sliding onto or off a note, the amount and speed depending on how far and fast your pitch bend control is moved from its central position. The pitch range of the control can be adjusted on the synth. For this piece, pitch bend of one semitone will be sufficient.

The sign ⌐ is commonly used to show an upward pitch bend. If it appears before a note it indicates sliding up to the written pitch. Placed during or after a note, it implies bending this note upwards. The same principle applies to the downward pitch bend sign ⌐. Co-ordinating pitch bend with playing the keyboard needs some practice. In particular, when bending into a note, you will need room to move the control before the note starts.

OTHER CONTROLLERS

The use of aftertouch (A), modulation (M) and breath controller (BC) is denoted in the score by ∿∿∿∿. These indications should only be taken as suggestions – a controller that sounds good on one voice may be completely unacceptable when used on another.

MIDI volume control data is particularly useful if you want to get louder through a single note, as in bars 29-30. It can be transmitted from a foot pedal or, like all other controller information, step written into the sequence.

INPUTTING CONTROLLER DATA

Most players find it simplest to operate the controllers as they are playing, recording this data automatically along with the rest of the sequence. It is also possible to record the track straight, and then to add controller information a second time round on a spare track set to the same MIDI channel.

Methods of writing controller data vary slightly between sequencers: check your manual for details.

Some sequencers allow controller data to be edited by dragging the mouse over a graphic display:

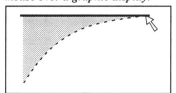

Another alternative is to step write control data, in the same way that notes can be step written. Instead of pitches, controller names or numbers are used: modulation is generally controller 1, breath control is 2 and volume is 7. Similarly, in place of velocities, a number representing the amount of movement of the controller can be input. Most controllers accept a range of values from 0 to 127, although pitch bend often has a resolution of more than plus or minus 8000. Here are some possible values for bending the note in bar 16 – this bend should take no more than an eighth-note to complete:

-8000, -6200, -4700, -3400, -2200, -1300, -700, -250, 0 (note now at pitch).

When step writing control information, it is important to set the final value to zero, otherwise the controller will remain in effect for the rest of the track. Controller 7, however, should be reset to 127 after use to restore maximum volume potential to the channel. Remember that the impact of a *crescendo* will depend upon the notes' original velocity level and the decay characteristics of the voice, as much as on the effect of this controller. In this, as in all cases, MIDI controller information doesn't alter the status of the original note.

Recording

Record the backing first, repeating the last four bars often enough to provide a fade ending. Split the solo part between two tracks, voiced for **sax** and **oboe**, making sure that all MIDI filters are switched off. Remember that sax voices are usually extremely velocity sensitive – minor variations in key pressure can produce startling changes in tone. Apart from cosmetic work on any truly outrageous bumps, however, the solo parts will sound more natural and spontaneous if they are not quantized too heavily.

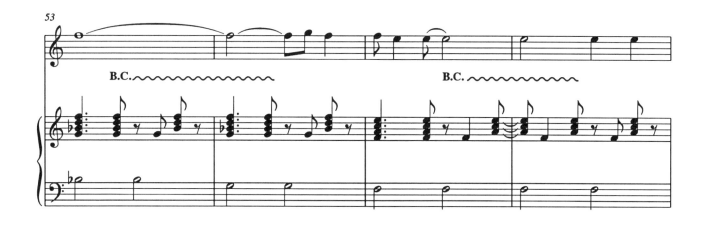

Try transposing the finished sequence down 4 semitones, into the key of A-flat.

DRUM TRACK

The drum track consists of a single-bar pattern that starts in bar 31 and can be repeated for the rest of the sequence. It should, of course, fade with the other tracks at the end.

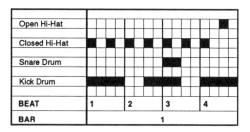

Developments

The following sequence features a vibes solo. The cool jazz style needs a pretty hot technique to play live on the keyboard, but it is short enough to make it worth step writing or recording very slowly.

The descending sixteenth-note triplets in bar 12 form a **chromatic** scale – solos of this kind are generally full of chromatic passing notes which can make the part feel somewhat remote from the underlying chord pattern. The backing tracks are therefore very straight to compensate for this, although the bass and guitar parts do occasionally cut loose.

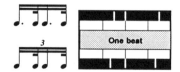

Notice how the backing often includes the dotted note figure shown *upper left* when the vibes part is playing triplets. In practice this would usually be played with triplet note lengths (*lower left*) to match the swing feel of the solo part and to prevent tiny hiccups in the rhythm.

Make the strings part super-*legato* in this piece, overlapping each note by as much as a quarter-note, to sound smooth and syrupy. It will almost certainly have to be transposed up two octaves, as indicated by *15ma* in the score. Notice that the main melody in bars 9-12 and 21-24 is printed on the strings stave to save space. This needs to be recorded on a separate track, voiced for **trumpet**.

In bars 25-26 a gradual slowing down (*rit.*) will stop the ending from sounding too abrupt. This can be done, as in Sequence 6, by manually setting a new tempo, perhaps at each half beat. Many sequencers also allow you to record tempo information using the mouse while the music is playing – this may provide a smoother result. Check your manual for tempo recording options.

With so much rhythmic interest in the other tracks a very simple drum pattern will suffice for the whole of bars 1-24. Don't use it during the final two-bar *rit.* though, or you will create the effect of a train grinding into the terminus.

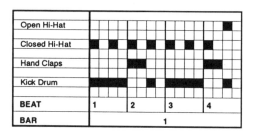

Sequence 14
Ballet Nights

Sequencing orchestral music offers the challenge of using synthesized voices to produce a realistic acoustic sound. Both pieces in this chapter rely heavily on the subtle use of dynamic (velocity) variety together with careful attention to articulation (note-lengths). Editing on the sequencer in this case will perform much the same rôle as a conductor – carefully grading the volume while ensuring that the rhythm is absolutely precise and consistent across several parts simultaneously.

Danse des Mirlitons

This is the first part of a dance from Tchaikovsky's famous ballet "The Nutcracker", featuring three flutes (a *mirliton* is a kind of toy flute) supported by strings. There are also short solos for bassoon and cor anglais.

SAMPLING

Synth string voices, in particular, can be notoriously difficult to make sound realistic. The most convincing voices will have been synthesized using a process known as **sampling**. This involves digitally analysing the actual sound made by a live performer, taking as many as 48,000 measurements per second. A similar sampling rate is also used by commercial CD recordings.

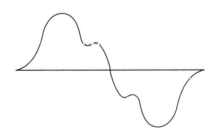

Original Sound Wave

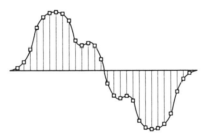

Sampling measures the wave at regular intervals

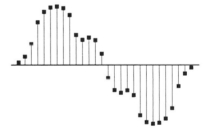

The wave can later be reformed from the stored values

A really comprehensive set of string samples, covering the entire pitch range, can easily take up all the memory of a micro-computer. Using this amount of memory for just one voice is far beyond the capacity of most synths, although many manage to produce a very acceptable sound by clever manipulation of a limited amount of sample data. The string parts in this piece should work reasonably well using any type of string voice, particularly as the music is *staccato* and fast moving.

SCORING

Some sequencers offer an option to match quantize. After getting one part right, this will allow you to line up the rhythms and velocities of other parts against it.

Pizzicato is an instruction for string players to pluck, rather than to bow (**Arco**). On a synth, an acceptable substitute is to change to the plucked sound of a guitar or harp voice.

The orchestral layout of this piece is relatively simple. The three flute parts share the same rhythm throughout. Record slowly, initially leaving the grace notes out, as this will enable you to quantize note-starts to sixteenth-notes. It is well worth spending time on getting note-lengths absolutely precise – the whole style of this piece depends upon articulation. As a rule of thumb, *staccato* notes should last for only half their notated lengths.

The bass part is *pizzicato* and can be played by any clear bass voice. This part would sound an octave lower than written when played by the double basses of an orchestra. The two short solos for bassoon and cor anglais need to be extremely *legato* and should be taken by a double-reed voice, such as **oboe**, with added breath controller (or modulation).

The three string parts follow a similar scheme to the flutes. You will need a program change after the first chord from a plucked sound (possibly **acoustic guitar**) to a bowed **string** sound, then back to *pizzicato* before the last note.

VELOCITIES

Variations in volume will play a major part in the success of this music. Some possible velocity levels are suggested by the ringed numbers. These are marked with arrows when followed by a *crescendo* or *diminuendo*. The actual values will depend upon the responsiveness of the voices you use. Changes in volume can be handled quite easily as quantize options – the only place you might want to use MIDI volume controller is on the bassoon solo in bars 7-10.

SCORE READING

Unlike songs, where the accompaniment is usually reduced to just treble and bass lines, orchestral scores show the parts played by every instrument. To save space they are often printed in very small format (miniature score) and generally omit complete staves where instruments are silent. Here, three string parts come in for the first time at bar 25 and the double-reed stave disappears.

Notice the changes between treble and bass clef in the viola part. The pitch range of this instrument encompassses both clefs.

The bass and flute parts in bars 27-39 can be copied (after editing) from bars 3-15. Similarly, the string parts in bars 36-40 can be copied from bars 28-32.

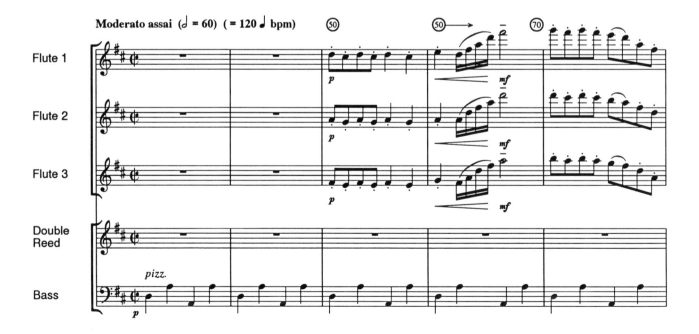

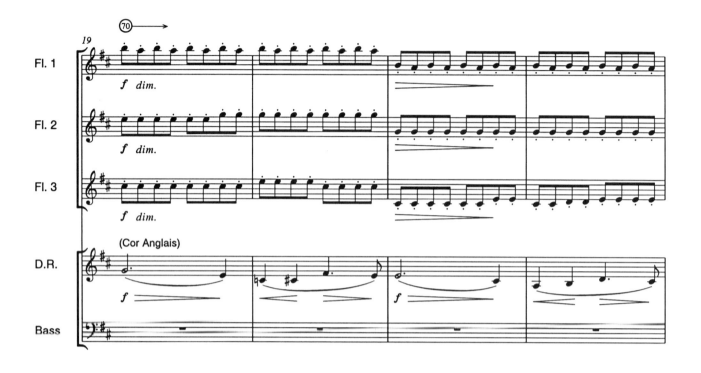

TRANSPOSING INSTRUMENTS

The opening music of this piece by Schubert is printed *overleaf* exactly as it appears in orchestral score. Notice that the clarinet and horn parts appear to be in a different key from the rest of the orchestra. This is because these instruments are built so that they automatically transpose. Thus, a clarinet in B-flat will sound the note B-flat whenever a C is played – and all of its other notes will correspondingly sound two semitones below their written pitch. Similarly, horns in F sound seven semitones lower than the written notes (*ie* F sounds when C is played). These tracks will therefore need to be transposed down on the sequencer before playback.

ALTO CLEF

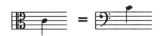

The pitch of a viola is too low to fit comfortably on the treble clef. Rather than alternating between treble and bass clefs as in the previous sequence, viola parts conventionally use the **alto clef**, where C4 ("middle C") is on the middle line of the stave. Viola players eventually get used to working with this mid-range clef, but others may appreciate the following bass clef version:

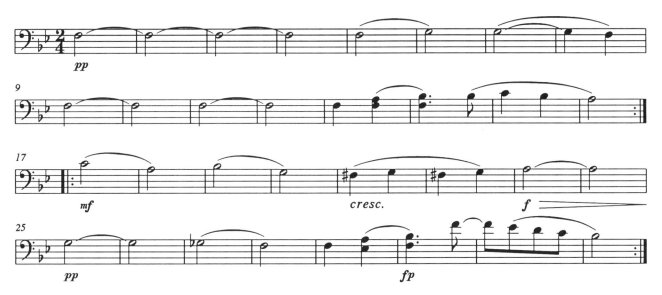

The *diminuendo* in bars 23-24 needs a controller velocity change from, say, 100 down to 40. Remember to set it back to 127 at the start of bar 25 or subsequent notes will be robbed of their full velocity potential.

There is no need, of course, to attempt to reproduce exactly the orchestral texture. At such a slow tempo, we were unable to find a completely satisfactory string or clarinet sound and eventually produced the following voicing:

Track 1	Flutes stave	**Vibes**	Channel 2
Track 2	Oboes stave	**Oboe**	Channel 3
Track 3	Clarinets stave	**Soft Brass**	Channel 4
Track 4	Bassoons stave	**Soft Brass**	Channel 4
Track 5	Horns stave	**Soft Brass**	Channel 4
Track 6	Violin 1 stave	**Pan Flute**	Channel 5
Track 7	Violin 2 stave	**Strings**	Channel 6
Track 8	Viola stave	**Choir**	Channel 7
Track 9	'Cello/Bass stave	**Acoustic Bass**	Channel 8

If you have a synth that is capable of more than eight multi-timbral voices, Tracks 3 to 5 will obviously not need to share a voice or channel.

Sequence 15
Finale – *The Muppets' Theme*

This last sequence will fully test the resources of an eight-voice multi-timbral synth. Possible program changes are given for each track, as are basic suggestions for articulation and volume. The rest is up to you!

Index

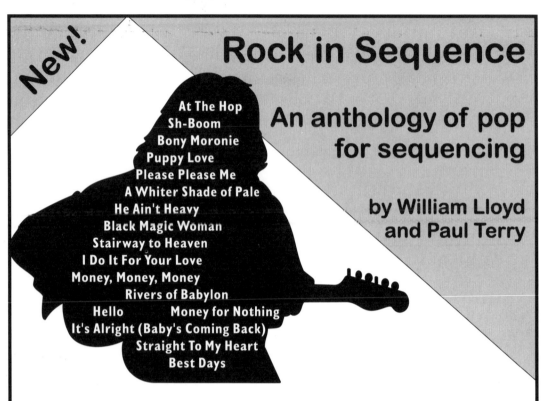
23 NOV 2000 28711/4